T0077910

BETRAYED!

A TRUE-LIFE STORY OF INTERNATIONAL BUSINESS AND GREED

MARIANNE PALEY

authorHOUSE®

AuthorHouse™ UK
1663 Liberty Drive
Bloomington, IN 47403 USA
www.authorhouse.co.uk
Phone: UK TFN: 0800 0148641 (Toll Free inside the UK)
        UK Local: (02) 0369 56322 (+44 20 3695 6322 from outside the UK)

Published by AuthorHouse 07/04/2022

ISBN: 978-1-6655-9882-8 (sc)
ISBN: 978-1-6655-9881-1 (e)

CONTENTS

FOREWORD

Traditionally, there are seven 'Deadly Sins', but truly a glaring omission is one that resonates deep within our moral compass and is the most remembered from historical, religious and personal experience: betrayal.

Think of Judas Iscariot's denunciation of Jesus; Brutus whose treachery is remembered from the disappointment felt by Julius Caesar in his heartfelt cry "Et tu, Brute?"; or Samson and Delilah, whose seduction led to his downfall. We all seem to feel the betrayal of trust the most keenly. Some might try to excuse this injustice inflicted by man on his fellow man with motives of fear, ambition, vengeance, or greed, but we have sympathy and empathy for the wronged that touches us deep within our psyche.

In more recent times the long-suffering, "fragrant" Mary Archer stood by her man despite his acknowledged affairs, while the public sided with Diana over Charles, proving that to many, loyalty (or, put another way, the absence of betrayal) remains the most valued trait we look for in our family and friends. Even in the wider world of the workplace or in government circles, where underhand conduct is seemingly excused by the phrase 'All's fair in love and war', we do not easily turn a blind eye to it or allow it to go unsanctioned.

Vengeance is mine, sayeth the Lord, and this retelling of events is not intended to circumvent this happening in the unlikely event the guilty are punished for their actions by some higher power, nor should the ensuing words be assumed in any way to signify the bestowing of forgiveness.

Despite the passing of some 12 years since my own discovery of this betrayal by our friends and business partners, my feelings of hurt and injustice are still as deep as in those last fateful days. What follows is how the dream of building our own business and which succeeded through dint of blood, sweat and tears, then when at the apogee of its success, having done all the heavy lifting, it seemed we were considered surplus to requirements and so greed led to betrayal when we were stabbed in the back in an unexpected and shocking underhand manner.

It is still intensely painful to re-live these events in order to tell the story of the relationships that were tainted irrevocably by the actions of my erstwhile friends and business colleagues. The intention is not to publicly denigrate the ex-partners; if they happen to read this, they know who they are, and after the passage of time, I doubt that anyone else will recognise the parties involved or even care. The pieces of silver have been counted, and the telling of my personal story will not change anything. They have nicely profited and made their way on to other concerns, and I do not have any power to hurt them financially. Nor is it likely to sully any reputations; in the recounting of events, I have been at pains to ensure that the "guilty parties" have not been named directly. I am sure that they all, unlike me, sleep soundly at night believing they did nothing wrong as indeed legally they did not. You can judge for yourselves how they would sit on your own moral compass.

I only hope that my story is an interesting and salutary tale, and perhaps that it will serve as a warning to others to be careful not to make the mistake of confusing friendship with business.

More than this, my wish is that through the process of sharing, and in the laying down of the words, in this tablet not of stone, but on paper and digital form, it may bring some cathartic peace and finally lay to rest the demons that still haunt my dreams.

CHAPTER ONE

"I HAD A FARM IN AFRICA"

This chapters' title has been appropriated from one of my favourite films, with due acknowledgement to Karen Blixen, and although I did not have a farm, but rather a business, it seemed as appropriate as any to start my story. Better, I think, than "Once Upon a Time" (as this is more horror story than fairy tale). Graham Greene wrote that, "A story has no beginning or end; arbitrarily one chooses that moment of experience from which to look back or from which to look ahead". So, I begin in Africa – the home of the Angora or Mohair Goat.

It is a little-known fact that the Mohair Goat's hair (often erroneously described as "wool"), – is a superb fibre, being naturally imbued with anti-bacterial, anti-abrasive and warmth preserving properties making it infinitely superior to the more usual and mundane common or garden sheep's wool or fleece. I mention these facts, as they will become helpful as my tale unfolds. These properties in the fibres can only be fully appreciated when viewed down a microscopes' lens; unlike wool and human hair, which has a series of scales akin to the skin of a fish, mohair is shiny, and so, if you will forgive my crude description, it means that "shit doesn't stick to it". Put another way, if a garment such as the humble sock has this included as a principal component, it not only never smells, as it repels the nasty sweat bacteria from adhering easily and multiplying, but it is also wonderfully comfortable to wear for long periods, being so smooth in contact with the skin. It therefore has gained popularity over the years and is known for being added to hiking socks.

Why does my story start here? Well, my journey, really began many years before when I first met my talented husband, who can gauge the quality or microns (thickness) of any natural fibre by chewing a small piece as a sort of party trick.

He was just 21 at the time we met; having been apprenticed from the age of 16 in a textile mill in West Yorkshire, he had learnt pretty much everything there is to know about the manufacture of yarns.

His specialism was in natural fibres, from the farming of the raw materials, be they from a vegetable origin such as cotton or flax (used in linen production), to the animal-derived sources, including wool and all the other more exotic ones such as angora, cashmere and the lovely mohair. Having declined to follow his father into the mechanical engineering firm (principally, I think, due to some internal family politics), it was a logical career choice to begin his employment and career at the mill, which was within a handy walking distance close to the village of his birth.

He followed the fibres through the entire process from being picked, shorn, or simply combed, as the more expensive fibres were painstakingly collected, through to the process of spinning the natural or synthetic fibres. These were later to be transformed into knitting wools and other textiles, including carpeting, upholstery, home furnishings and materials destined for garments, and a myriad of others, depending on the type, quality and properties in the desired finished article.

Our paths first crossed in a small Yorkshire pub close to the mill, which at that time was one of the last remaining British yarn spinners majoring in the manufacture of mohair. This rather old-fashioned material, beloved by the 70's hippies and punks for their iconic hairy jumpers, among other familiar staples such as the cosy travel blanket or throw, had a small, rather niche following, so it is here that the yarn really began (please excuse the pun).

Introduced by an old school friend of his, I was initially unimpressed, being six years his senior, and at 27 considering myself something of a sophisticate and destined for greatness, (such is the arrogance of youth). I remember looking him up and down with little interest at our first encounter and dismissing him as a potential partner in one head-to-toe appraising glance, rather akin to the way a farmer might appraise a prize bull at market.

However, another chance encounter came about when having a drink with a friend in his local public house as he played on one of the then popular games machines. After spying his rather pert buttocks, I rather provocatively made a rather crude complimentary comment, and so the chase was on.

It was a rather protracted and torrid ten years courtship; as our respective friends and relatives commented, we were "like chalk and cheese" in almost every respect. So, it was something of a miracle that we ended up even dating after that less than auspicious first encounter. I was considered rather "posh" as I still retained my "upper class accent" from my army officer's daughter upbringing. And with my newly awarded Business Studies degree, I thought I was quite a catch for some similar professional at the upper end of the social scale: perhaps a doctor or lawyer or titled landed gentry man. However, I was always contrary in nature (something I later recognised as a rather fatal flaw), and this was allied to somewhat of a self-destructive streak. When faced with the sensible or obvious choice, I nearly always did the opposite of what was expected and so seemed to be cursed with a sort of Hari-Kiri death wish tendency which followed me at every crossroads in life.

Consequently, it should maybe come as no surprise that I reverted to this pattern with this most crucial and important decision. I eventually had to choose between the two suitors I had at the time; on the one hand a very handsome boy whose father owned or ran some massive Petro-chemical concern in Sweden, (rather akin to the *Some Like it Hot* Tony Curtis, to whom the Marilyn Munroe character gravitated, believing him to be a multi-millionaire magnate of the Shell oil conglomerate), and on the other this rather gauche, working class textile apprentice-cum-manager possessing a strong regional accent and no fancy airs and graces. Bizarrely, and much to everyone's surprise, I chose to continue my relationship with the latter. Maybe I had been charmed on our first date after he had begged my friend so much to allow him to take me out. I had reluctantly agreed, as the "safe" choice, to let him take me to the pictures to see *A Room with a View.*

On that occasion he had picked me up in his ancient battered Series 1 Land Rover, which not only had no heating, but I was also advised I had to operate the windscreen wipers by hand. To cap the indignity, I discovered that I had to kick open the passenger door in order to get out. I was not overly impressed at the time!

As fate would have it, it was after that less than romantic start that he played his hand just right. At the end of the date, after we had talked throughout the entire film, (no doubt annoyingly to the other cinema goers), he refused to even attempt to proffer a goodnight kiss, and so unwittingly he piqued my contrary nature. This made me decide to bring him completely under my spell, and so I agreed to continue the relationship. His case was also unwittingly aided and abetted when I heard of his mothers' comment; she had asked him in a negative manner, "Just how old is this woman you are seeing?" (Perhaps expecting some cunning divorcée with a gaggle of illegitimate brats in tow). This also made me more determined to keep seeing him.

Whatever the reasons, after a very long lead time from dating to reluctant engagement, to appropriate a line from one of the best-loved Bronte sisters' works (I lived only a few miles from Haworth). "Reader, I married him". He eventually persuaded me to walk down the aisle at the comparatively late age of 35.

I had vociferously resisted the very thought of marriage as it was never my goal in life to "just" be a housewife or, God forbid, a mother. My own had inured me against this by stating repeatedly, and more than a little bit hurtfully, that in her opinion, "children ruin your life".

We did have an amazing honeymoon in Egypt though. A video producer was so taken with my entrance to the iconic Old Winter Palace Hotel in Luxor wearing one of my dramatic signature hats that he decided there and then to offer to film us in some various sequences for a promotional video for the hotel he had been commissioned to make. This included a specially commissioned balloon ride over the Valley of the Kings, starting at sunrise at Hatshepsut's temple, where, as the dawn cast a beautiful ethereal pink glow over the temple, we were greeted by the awe-inspiring sight of our midnight blue and silver balloon being inflated with dramatic flames emanating from bursts from their burners. Being truly afraid of heights, with teeth chattering from fear and excitement in equal measure, the slow ascent into the air was something that everyone should experience. However, I was determined, despite my fear, to go through with it. (Due to a terrorist incident some years later when some tourists were shot at this location, balloon take-offs there are now banned, so it was truly a once in a lifetime opportunity.)

After we drifted peacefully over the ancient burial sites with a bird's eye view of the enormity and majesty of the tomb sites, we landed in the sandy desert after being chased on our descent by a host of excited village children; they had been delighted by the spectacle of a couple in one midnight blue and silver balloon being filmed from a second. Once safely landed, we were treated to a breakfast of salmon, scrambled eggs and champagne, served to us personally by the chef of the Hilton. This had all been set up in advance for us, complete with white tablecloth and silver ware. I suppose that everyone's honeymoons are special, but the addition of the filming and the additional free excursions added a certain frisson to it.

Rather annoyingly, my husband was initially resistant to taking the offer up at all, but I embraced it totally, wearing each of my carefully chosen outfits and accompanying hats and immersing myself in romantic dreams of a film-star's existence.

I cannot resist mentioning that, on Day One of the "shoot", as we were filmed in the specially arranged carriage and horses arriving at the hotel in style, I played my amateur dramatics role to the full, waxing lyrical about the thrilling salmon pink exterior of the hotel as we pulled up to the steps outside. Enthusiastically and reverentially, I breathed the words, "What an amazing colour, do you think it's sandstone?' This improvised line was meant to add a bit of whimsical romance to the clip, but, to my annoyance and shame, my no-nonsense, phlegmatic husband replied in his strong Yorkshire accent, "Noooo, its PAINT!" …Arrghhhh.

It reminded me of the iconic advertisement from around that era, when the beautiful, elegantly dressed model, Lorraine Chase, was asked by a handsome gentleman, "Were you truly wafted here from paradise?" only for her to reply in an unrefined cockney accent " Nahhh, mate, Luton Airport".

We had a wonderful time, though, and were promised after production and editing was completed, we would be sent our own copy of the filming as our own special memory of that time.

Now, back to earth with a bump in England, we cut to just a short while later, after that incredible high point of our lives, to the distressing time when the decimation of the UK textile industry began caused multiple redundancies in that sector. It had been deemed politically necessary to allow free market trade, and so began the demise of that proud and skilled British craftsmanship, dispensed with in favour of purchasing goods made overseas at the much-reduced prices due to the cheaper labour costs abroad.

With the take-over of the small mohair spinning subsidiary by its larger parent company, my husband endured the threat and eventual reality of redundancy, not once, but twice, as initially he was one of the few personnel absorbed by the parent company in a larger city location, involving a long commute. Then, as the industry was squeezed mercilessly by the increasing need to cut more and more costs to be competitive, he was once again put out in the cold. This was after some extremely challenging and stressful years, during which Thatcher's yuppie boom and massive increases in mortgage interest rates meant that we had struggled to make ends meet. Now, prompted by an employment opportunity which would allow him to remain in the industry he loved, we moved to Port Elizabeth, South Africa, the home of the angora mohair goat.

This remarkable animal subsists miraculously, as a farmer once succinctly put it, on the miles and miles of "bugger all" that was called "The Karoo", an area of arid rocky landscape in the Eastern Cape far away from the more fertile, greener coastline where most of the major cities are located. If you ever have occasion to look at what grows there at first-hand and close-up, you will indeed see that generally it consists of nothing but an expanse of barren desert stretching as far as the horizon, bereft of anything that could remotely be called grass or indeed anything that could be considered edible at all.

When we arrived in Port Elizabeth, or PE as the locals called it, it was still in the immediate aftermath of the ending of the apartheid regime, so these were exciting and memorable (not to say dangerous) times. The troubled transition of Mandela's new governing party was still being played out in various power struggles in this period of adjustment. There were all sorts of peculiar transitions going on, with positive discrimination, corruption and nepotism rife as attempts were made to balance the wide gap between the standards of living and cultures of the white English and Afrikaner South Africans, and the Xhosa and Zulus and myriad of other native ethnic tribes in this rainbow country.

The inevitable power struggle and the white echelons' fear of being over-run was very real, as they mainly occupied extremely well-appointed houses in nice suburbs. Their concern was made worse by the expectations and hopes of the local population who, fired up by the ending of the oppressive regime, and with some of their own now in positions of power, expected that immediately they would be moving out of their shanty townships and straight into the white homes to claim their rightful (as they saw it) entitlement to an opulent and more equitable way of life.

It was a regular, if not slightly comical sight, to see a group of workmen attending to some road repairs where the scene was like this: – 1x white "boss" leant up against a vehicle smoking (the supervisor); 6 or 8 black workmen stood around a hole looking down or chatting amongst themselves and sharing a joke with one of their team who had been assigned to be the one down the hole digging. This was part of the plan to positively get more people into work and onto the employment ladder; however, as I alluded to above, there were all sorts of dodgy dealings going on. Anyone employed in any management position could use this for their own and their relatives' and friend's advancement. These positive discrimination appointees were employed, not based on any fair interview or on merit. They could often be seen sitting at desks at town halls or government buildings with nothing in front of them and apparently nothing to do. Sometimes they were just employed to point or refer customers to another desk where a trained white employee did the work. Worse still, I sometimes heard talk of jobs being given to the highest bidder (or bribe as we would call it). However, it is hard to be judgemental after the horrors of apartheid, and it is probably only what happens in other countries no matter what the nationality or colour of a person's skin. It was just seen as part of the transition process and so most just shrugged their shoulders and turned a blind eye to it.

As the spectre of apartheid was still alive and well, particularly in the Eastern Cape, where we had settled, rather than the more cosmopolitan Western Cape where Cape Town was located with the more civilised Stellenbosch wine hinterland regions, this made for a rather strange atmosphere. For a relatively sophisticated, English Business school graduate, marketing consultant and then IT professional, it was like stepping back into the 60s, especially when compared to the (while admittedly still chauvinistic), 80s and 90s in the UK, where Margaret Thatcher had proven that women could get to the top through their own efforts. However, it seemed in South Africa that the role of the female Boer descendants was chiefly to find a suitable husband and then to look after his needs by making satisfying meals. Childbearing and rearing seemed to be their primary other raison d'etre. I was shocked on one occasion by an example of this rather homely attitude to "women's work" when I heard that this could involve such delights as hand-sewing one's offspring's undergarments. This struck me as being a rather comical and indeed bizarre notion, especially as my first job after graduating from my degree, was in the buying department of a lingerie manufacturer and it was due to the introduction of a co-worker and friend I made there that I had met my husband to be.

One of the perks of the job at the lingerie company was to be able to obtain, at extremely low cost, some fantastic underwear from the factory shop, which had been put to one side as 2nds, or slightly imperfects, and so consequently could not be sent on to the specialist and department stores who had ordered them. I therefore had lots of beautiful lingerie, complete with various matching bra, knicker and suspender belts, cami-knickers & French knicker sets, some of them in pure silk and expensive lace and in a myriad of colours, as each season our Managing Director visited the textile shows with his in-house designers to check out what the in-vogue colours to produce for the forthcoming year were.

Coming from the UK where, as everyone knows, M&S was the go-to for all self-respecting persons' underwear purchases and, of course, most people did not have occasion to avail themselves of the nice "2nds" from the factory shop as I did. I remember once embarrassingly describing them to some new people I had been introduced to, after having had one or two glasses of wine, and happily telling them that I wore "second-hand" underwear, which of course is entirely not the same thing. They were no doubt wondering how I could have had the poor taste to procure "pre-loved" underwear... As these things go, I only recalled this as a sort of shameful flashback the next morning and cringed at what they must have thought of me.

Having said that, I do remember when, as small children, my mother made us some clothes using some second-hand coats purchased from charity shops or thrift shops (as they were then called). She was talented at design and sewing, and she cleverly made these up into little skirts and bolero jackets, which she then hand-embroidered with little flowers and added imitation pearls at the centres of each to be greatly admired by all who saw them. However, that was many years ago, and at a time when my parents had had little money for new outfits for three growing daughters. It was not in the affluent 1990's, where to make one's own clothes was seen more as a hobby than a necessity.

We supplied most of the high street department stores (but we notably did not supply that staple of British underwear M&S). There was a very practical reason for this (and recollections of this strategy would inform my later intransigence about reserving stock for one "special" customer after starting our company in America). At that time, as a supplier to this well-respected retailer, meant that they could basically dictate everything you did, as they had a reputation for selling only high-quality products to maintain. This dangerously meant that you usually ended up being their sole supplier. As you can imagine, this "all eggs in one basket" strategy could end badly. I felt it was very smart of my MD to avoid this and hence we had total autonomy over the production processes. Instead, we supplied many customers including the likes of Debenhams, Co-op, and several fashion chains like Chelsea Girl, Pippa-Dee and others (now sadly almost all long gone from the high street). We even supplied an important French lingerie distributor, who, as a major customer, often came over and visited the production and design department. As they spoke little or no English, (or declined to), this meant that my cohort in the Buying Office, who became a dear friend, had been employed partly for her excellent French; and she exclusively looked after their account. I had studied German initially, but after moving "up north" had been sent to a school who only taught French as a foreign language. As a result of that inconvenient move, I was always badly behind and the dunce of the class. I was often berated by the teacher for pronouncing the words in a "German" way. (Those of you that have had occasion to speak both languages, will know that the Germanic way is to enunciate every single syllable, while the Gallic fashion is to omit many of the word endings).

It was a pity, as, having lived as a small child in various German Army postings, I had acquired through some sort of osmosis, a good accent and had previously been the top of my class in that all too short and important first year of learning a new language. C'est la vie…

However, remembering those years in my first job at the "knicker factory" as I irreverently called it, makes me feel nostalgic. They were, in the main, fun filled days, redolent of the *Coronation Street* sort of camaraderie (you may know that this soap opera features an underwear sewing mill). It is at this point; I digress down memory lane with some anecdotal stories, which I hope you will enjoy, and in the hope that they will help you understand how these experiences fatefully set the scene of my life to come and help understand what happens later in the book. Even after all these years they make me laugh out loud, so I hope they do the same for you.

The first story could be straight out of one of the then not-dreamed-of Bridget Jones books and is from my very first job interview at the company.

To set the stage, I will share a couple of salient points; one was that I had a penchant for hats even back then, as you may have guessed from my film debut on honeymoon. (Even now have about 30 different styles and colours scattered about my bedroom, squeezed in on tops of various cupboards, including some special ones like the infamous wide brimmed one from Egypt which I keep sentimentally in a special hat box purchased to keep it safe through our many house moves). I also inherited my grandmother's love of fashionable clothes, and specifically for smart skirt-suits. She had run a successful fashion boutique in her day, and my mother said she was always "borrowing" her clothes, once recounting an occasion when she had stopped the traffic on Preston High Street when wearing one of these outfits, a particularly fetching number appropriated from her mother's wardrobe, and carrying a huge bouquet of flowers. She recalls that as she waited to cross over the road, the traffic simply came to a complete standstill so they could let her across and admire her as she did so.

In turn, I had managed to borrow one of her nice Jacques Vert black suits, a smart white blouse, and topped it off with my own black floppy brimmed Fedora which I thought would be perfect for attending interviews in a stylish fashion. I reasoned that this was totally appropriate for the occasion, as the interview was at a clothing company, which had its own design facility, complete with its very own temperamental Italian fashion designer. I fancifully imagined that, when she was not designing lingerie or jetting back and forth to Paris or Milan, she would be driving her sporty Alpha Romeo around at breakneck speed, complete with some stylish Isadora Duncan scarf blowing behind her.

To complete the fashionable yet professional look that I was wanting to present, I had purchased a black and gold Parker fountain pen. I thought it would set the right tone of a serious and well-educated intelligent woman, and to cap it off, as a graduation present, my father had bought me a massive black briefcase, which I took it along, although it seemed a bit large to hold my pen, notepad and copy of my CV.

After announcing my arrival incredibly early at the reception hatch, having feared I might be late driving to this new location (in those days there was no sat-nav), I was seated in the lobby area and told to wait until I was called. There were two doors on either side of the reception area and a toilet that I was grateful to be able to use as I was extremely nervous, it being my first interview.

As I sat there, someone emerged from one of the side doors and wandered through the reception area. Glancing sideways, she spotted this tiny black-clad figure complete with a hat fit for a funeral. I nodded and smiled at her in what I hoped was a confident and winning manner, wondering if this was one of the potential bosses. As I did, I noted her do a double take as if she could not quite believe what she had seen.

After what seemed to be several long seconds with her gaze, which was a little unnerving in its intensity, she disappeared back through the door she had just come through, as if she had forgotten something. Then, only a minute or so later, I noticed another person casually passing through from the same door she had just exited through and taking a surreptitious and sidelong glance at me. This was quickly followed by yet another person, and then what seemed to turn into a bit of a steady stream of passers-by. I supposed that, in this small, sleepy northern town, they had probably rarely seen anyone wearing such a hat unless they were at a wedding or some more sombre event. Then I started to think maybe it had been a bit of a bad idea, but I was stuck with my decision. It was too late to try and stuff it into my briefcase and have it ruined in the process.

So, I continued to just smile back as each onlooker passed through, while feeling increasingly uncomfortable. I was therefore relieved when I was finally called through for my interview by the MD's personal assistant so the peep show could come to an end.

I was shown into a grand wood panelled office. Seated behind the desk to greet me was a short, boyish-looking man, who introduced himself as the IT Systems Manager. The nice young PA, after offering me a tea or coffee, seated herself slightly to the side but at a desk behind the one he was sitting at, and gathered up her pad and pen ready to take some notes.

Once seated in front of the large desk, I placed my rather enormous briefcase by the side of my chair, and out of it retrieved my special Parker fountain pen which had been newly charged with blue ink (my parents had advised was the only colour for letter writing). Then I got out my own small, lined pad and placed it on my lap. I knew it was important to ask questions and make notes to show I seriously wanted the job.

The interview started out in what I supposed was the usual fashion. I do not recall what was asked but presume it was something about why I wanted the job, and what I thought I could bring to the company and role.

As I answered each question, I wanted to look as if I was pondering each carefully before framing my response, (as indeed I was), and so using my pen as a sort of indicator of this, I would pause and thoughtfully press it to my lips and chin, and then point it forwards as I answered in what I thought was a well-studied style. I would occasionally wave it about and write something down, saying things like, "Great point, I will make a note of that", or some such deliberate attempt to show I was enthusiastic and that despite my flowing blond locks, styled in the popular Farrah Fawcett tousled manner, I could be considered a serious and intelligent contender for the position.

At one point, peering upwards under the brim of my hat, I noticed that my interviewer seemed to be supressing a bit of a smile. It did not help as my chair was low down in typical subservient interviewee fashion. I was only 5 foot 3 inches (5 ft 3 and ¾ as, like all people conscious of small stature, I liked to make even the slightest increase count). It was something of a sore point with me as I was the shortest in my family by a good three inches, having even been outgrown by my younger sister from an early age, despite our two years' difference. My mother had quite tactlessly said it could have been the bottles of gin she drank while sat in in an extremely hot bath when she realised she was pregnant, to try and get rid of me. I was never sure if it was true or if it was me or my younger sister that had proved to be such an unwelcome interruption to her life, but it was a way of explaining why I was the shortest that seemed to ring true. Thinking it was perhaps to do with my hat, I said gaily, "Oh I am sorry, I suppose my hat does make me look a bit shifty; would you like me to take it off?" Immediately I though what a dumb thing to say but was keen to make light of it and get it "out there", but this only seemed to make him more amused, although he answered politely, "Oh, not at all, it's fine."

Appeased that this was OK, a few more questions followed. At each one I flicked my pen back and forth and sucked the end thoughtfully before writing a few more notes, but at this point my interviewer started to have a bit of a coughing fit, so the PA stood up and offered to get him some water and smiled at me kindly; she seemed to be a lovely person and to understand how nervous I was.

He declined the water, saying he was fine, and soon after that brought the interview to close. I reached out my hand to give the firm handshake I had been told always to give rather than the "flaccid sweaty paw approach".

I thanked both him and the PA for their time, relieved it had seemed to go quite well (although already thinking back that my "shifty" comment had perhaps been a little ill-advised). But all smiles, he shook my hand; and after I went out the door, he quickly closed it behind me, I thought perhaps I had talked too much as was my wont, and he was late for his next appointment.

But I was desperate to get out and back into the sanctuary of my old bashed up Renault, handed down third hand from my mother and sister, where I would be able to heave a huge sigh of relief that I had not completely cocked my interview up, and reflect on what had been said, with the key points while still fresh in my mind. Having plonked my briefcase onto the passenger seat, I sat down in the driver's seat. Then as was my customary habit, I popped down the sun visor to re-apply lipstick (my mother always said she simply could not drive without lipstick), so I always followed the same ritual.

But imagine my horror and dismay, when I realised that, in my attempt to look clever in my responses, I had managed to scribble blue ink all over

13

my face. Gahhhhh…. There was not just the odd little dot, but noooo, great big lines and blotches, especially around my mouth and chin, and my lips were quite blue from where I had briefly popped the end of the pen into my mouth for the extra thoughtful suck before replying to a particularly tricky question.

I thought, no wonder my interviewer had had such trouble keeping a straight face, and what an idiot he must have thought me. I berated myself for being such a complete and utter clown, and immediately assumed I wouldn't be offered the job after making such a debacle of myself.

My eyes watered at the humiliation; taking a tissue I spat on it and attempted to remove the ink, but in truth, I couldn't bear to hang around for long, so I drove off as quickly as possible, lest I hear the sound of the entire factory laughing at this sorry creature who thought she was so grand wearing a hat to an interview and had then managed to draw all over her own face with her pretentious fountain pen.

I had a flat tyre on the way home and a kind motorist stopped and helped me change it, so I was at least able to tell someone about my stupid gaffe and share my discomfort. He was exceedingly kind and said he was sure it would not affect my chances, and indeed, I was amazed when I was offered the job.

I was later told why I had been given the chance by my new (female), boss who was head of the Buying Office, (and incidentally one of the smartest people I have ever met). She said that the IT Manager had never laughed so much in his life. Later the nice PA told me that she had never heard him even giggle before (as actually he was a usually bit of a strait-laced type who took himself very seriously). She informed me that, sitting behind him throughout the interview, she had been able to see his shoulders shaking with the effort of not guffawing out loud. Maybe also suffering from being judged by his boyish looks and diminutive stature, he over-compensated with Napoleonic vigour and a severe manner lest anyone challenge his ability. I was feeling much better that I had not totally blown it by my foolishness, but my new boss then rather spoiled it, by adding, "But the other candidate was a right stiff, so we wouldn't have chosen him!"

In retrospect, I pondered that that he had had a lucky escape, as in an office staffed exclusively by women, added to a whole factory full of no-nonsense machinists, he might not have survived. I have heard tales where the "new boys" were taunted mercilessly, especially in this working-class environment with scathing, blunt northern humour.

One of these occasions as told me by my husband, who apprenticed at the tender age of 16 at the spinning mill, which also had a predominantly female workforce, he said that he had been the subject of many a prank. One classic instance that is still funny was the time he was told to go down to the workshop for a "Long Stand". Announcing on his arrival in the basement that this is what he had been sent for, after being stood there and ignored for about 20 minutes, and with no sign of any equipment appearing, he eventually realised that they were messing with him.

At the underwear facility, I could also imagine that not every young man is comfortable talking about double DD cup bras, big gussets and incontinence pants, (since, as well as the fancy lingerie, we made some of the latter for a customer in Finland, and of course took every opportunity to make jokes about it, in extremely poor taste).

But it proved to be a great first place to start work; although I was as green as grass and made lots of mistakes, for which I was brought up sharply, every day was interesting, though exhausting in the beginning. Like many graduates used to lying in on mornings before lectures started and having a lot of free "study" time, I really did not know what real work was.

I had managed to rent a small, terraced stone-built cottage in a village not far from the factory, but as the lounge downstairs opened directly onto the main road, without the benefit of a draught excluding porch, and it had flagged stone floors and just one small gas fire in the front room, it was absolutely freezing in winter. The insides of the windows would ice up with a thick layer of spangled crystals. Perhaps it's a legacy of having been born in a hot country, Singapore, when my father was posted there as an army officer, I hated the cold. Because of this aversion, I was often late for work as it was so hard to get up, as getting out of bed on a morning in sub-zero temperatures meant stepping onto a cold linoleum bedroom floor in bare feet. One morning, I remember I just threw myself bodily out of bed onto the floor as I had snoozed my alarm clock several times to put off that inevitable hideous shock of emerging from under my warm duvet into arctic conditions, but knew I was going to be late and in trouble if I did not get up right NOW.

After a while, I gave up sleeping upstairs; as I had bought a couple of sheepskin rugs to cover up the horrid brown stained sofa that came with the cottage, I threw them down in front of the gas-fire, and with duvet and pillow, slept there with the gas fire turned down low each night until the weather warmed up in spring. Also, being so close to the wild moors, it regularly snowed there, and the icy blasts that swept down from "Wuthering Heights" drove it in drifts into huge embankments at the side of the roads and fields; once embedded there, it took ages to thaw, remaining long into the new year. It was pretty to look at, but it was very cold.

I made a couple of close friends in the Buying Office at the lingerie company, but I am not sure I was ever a star performer in my initial role. Though I worked hard, most of the job was calculating numbers for accurate purchasing of materials, it was crucial to get this right, ensuring there wasn't too little material, ribbon, fabric, expensive lace, elastic, suspender ends, bra hooks and eyes purchased, nor was there an excess at the end of the production run due to over-ordering. As maths was never my strongest point and I was terrified of making a costly mistake, I would check and re-check the product sheets before submitting to the eagle eye of my clever boss, who could look at a page of numbers and sums and would be able to spot any anomaly within milliseconds with one stabbing accusatory finger, uttering the dreaded words "That's wrong".

But I was promoted after a time, to a role looking after the orders for the customers and being the go-between between sales and production teams to try and ensure that the shipping call-off matched the expected and actual orders. After time, I did manage to get good at customer service, but also had to become rather adept at "fibbing" to my accounts if production numbers were too low or stock was just not available for the projected times for call-off.

I hated doing it, but I and my opposite number in the same role were often forced to massage the figures that we sent through weekly to cover up any shortfall in the availability of the stock for call-off. We usually got away with it as often the customer would either not call it off over and above what we had produced. or did so when it was in final inspection mode, and therefore could be quickly finished off ready for delivery. So usually there was not too much danger of them discovering it was short against what had been promised. Where more was needed than what we were able to ship or complete immediately, we had a bit of notice from the receipt of the order to the expected delivery date to allow us to run through to the production floor and ask for the missing called-off styles and sizes to be hastily bumped up by switching the production line to make up the shortfall in time for the transport to be booked.

If the stock was not available for the delivery carrier to be booked in time, as a last resort, my colleague and I had a list of excuses or "untruths", we used in rotation; they were claims that we thought that our customers could not feasibly discover. We got away with lying as most people who lived "down south", already assumed anywhere north of Watford Gap to be the "frozen north", and I often did see snow from the start of October right through to the middle of April. If not snow, we used high winds or floods as an excuse for the delayed shipment. Sometimes we had to get a bit more creative, and, as Monty Python was at its height of popularity, we would joke that we should just say "The cat's eaten it".

Of course, we never said that, but as it was rather stressful trying to avoid a rollicking from our customers. If we were found out in a lie, the MD would have to answer some difficult questions, so it was a welcome stress relief to be able to make silly jokes; and it cemented our camaraderie colluding in making up believable excuses.

However, even that was to be sorely tested as changes were made whereby the accounts were more formally split between myself and my French-speaking colleague and friend. At this stage, we had to competitively claw for production capacity, not only from the local production plant where we were based (which mainly did the more complicated bra and suspender work), but also at two other manufacturing plants in Derbyshire (which mainly produced the knickers, or underpants as our American friends would call them). It was production of these lines that we were often behind on. I suppose one of the reasons would be for every bra purchased, at least two or three pairs of matching knickers were needed as, of course, all nice girls changed their underwear every day, but that would not always include one's bra.

It is also a consistent fact of business life that salespeople will never turn down an order for any reason as trivial as not having the capacity, and this is the reason why production people and salespeople usually do not get on. It's a conflict that is hard to parley, but I and my colleague were truly piggies in the middle, as we had to ensure that the customer was kept satisfied, without causing any meltdown on the production side by asking too much or continually changing the goalposts. In the beginning we had shared all the accounts, with the notable exception of the French one, and so had been able to discuss and juggle and come up with a compromise on what production lines we would ask for. This spirit of collaboration had previously worked quite well. However, the newly promoted IT manager (who had presided over my interview), who was now in charge of Operations, decided that we should be assigned our own accounts for which we would be individually responsible for ensuring that the production matched the order call-offs. This made our happy co-operation into a daily fight for resources which inevitably became a real source of conflict.

The production manager who managed both Derbyshire-based underwear plants, was a lovely, good-tempered and patient guy that we both liked very much. He got used to getting a call from me or my colleague from time to time when we realised, we had an order call-off that we were short on. However, whereas before the new regime was introduced, we would have had a chat about what we needed, now we were in a competitive situation where we would plead for our own customers' orders and ask for priorities to be changed in order to make up the shortfall. This was no easy thing to do for the beleaguered production and machine room supervisors, as the workers on the lines would be all set up with their sewing machines, with the requisite colour of threads loaded, all ready to commence work on their required target sizes on a line on a morning, only to be pulled off that and told to change to something else later that day. This chopping and changing was, of course, not very efficient. The poor production managers would get a call or fax from my colleague asking for some promised production, only to be contacted by me, sometimes even on the same day, with a request for something completely different.

I remember having a huge fallout with my opposite account manager one day; after receiving two conflicting requests close together from us, the manager of the underwear plant called to speak to me, complaining that he could not do both and what was he to do? I felt awful to have put him in this *Sophie's Choice* position of having to decide which of us he was to let down. I was faced with this dilemma and, not really knowing what to say, I rather unwisely said, "Oh sorry, we don't really know what we are doing here". This incensed my colleague so much she turned to me and said "Well, YOU may not know what you are doing, but I do".

She was understandably cross with me to have implied she was incompetent, so that was an extremely low point in the job and as the newly promoted systems controller increasingly seemed to work on a divide and conquer basis, it presaged the end of my time there. I thought I had best look for another job rather than increasingly be at loggerheads with my friend and colleague.

But I promised you another funny story, didn't I? This one was from the early days, when our French customer would occasionally come over for a visit to the factory. They were particularly important to us, as one of our largest key accounts, so there was always an aura of nervousness whenever we knew they were paying us a visit. The MD would roll out the red carpet for them, and special sandwiches and cakes would be brought in for their visit if they didn't have enough time to be taken out for lunch. We had a great canteen that made awesome sausage, bacon or egg buns at morning break time, but we felt sure our sophisticated Parisian customers would not appreciate them as we did.

In addition to the great canteen and the free breakfasts we enjoyed daily, one of the best parts of working in the "knicker factory" was that, to keep the workforce happy and entertained, a local radio station's music was piped through the entire factory floor and offices. On this occasion, as it was a few weeks before Christmas, we were all in a bit of a hyper-active and jolly mood. In the Buying Office, which we all still shared as a merry band of sisters (we were all female in there), we had been singing along with the cheery seasonal records as we worked away at our desks, and when the "Golden Oldie" Hour started in the late morning, "The Hippy-Hippy Shake" came on. For those of you who have no clue how it goes, it's a rollicking feelgood song which at the end of each verse concludes: "It's in the bag... pause for big crescendo... Wooooooahh, the hippy-hippy shake..."

So of course, we all got to this bit and ended up virtually shouting in unison at the end of each chorus – "Woooohhhh… the hippy-hippy shake…" All great fun.

My desk was situated right at the back of the room, facing away from the entrance door at the other end which led out onto the factory floor and the corridor to the offices. My colleague who looked after the French customer was seated opposite me looking down the room; as we performed the same job roles, our desks were placed facing each other in those early collaborative days.

Well, you might be able to predict what might came next. Just as the door opened and the esteemed and stylish French entourage who were over for one of their customary visits were ushered into the Buying office, "The Hippy-Hippy Shake" came to the last chorus and a big finish was called for. While everyone else clocked immediately the door opening and guests being shown in, I was blissfully ignorant of this event, facing as I did in the opposite direction, and with the sound of the door opening being masked by the radio station, just as everyone else fell silent, too late for me to be warned, I belted out massively loudly (especially obvious as not joined by anyone else in the vocal). – "Woooooohhh, THE HIPPY HIPPY SHAKE!"

Realising too late, I could only look as I saw my friend's shoulders shaking and face twitching, I sickeningly realised my mistake as she, while rather horrified by what had just happened, desperately tried not to crack up.

Looking beseechingly at her, willing it not to be as bad as I thought it was, as of course we were aware that it was THE visitor day, as she composed herself and got ready to meet the clients, I just hissed, mortified, "It's THEM, isn't it?" She just nodded, took a deep breath, and got up to greet them. I did not even dare turn round to witness the red-faced MD's discomfort and the bemused looks from the French contingent but wanted to get underneath the desk and kill myself. I didn't dare face the wrath of my big boss, as, while he was not a man without a sense of humour, I knew that he would not have been amused at my lack of timing and discretion.

Looking back at this, I would hope that anyone who has an ounce of humanity would think it a funny story. However, it seemed that after that, when I was desperate to get back into the good graces of my MD, who I respected a lot, whenever he was around, I was seen to be behaving like a complete nincompoop. I don't think it helped me trying so hard. The next time that he came down to our offices, just a few weeks later, as fate would have it, I had just dropped my pencil sharpener onto the floor. As he hove into view, on the way to speak to his account manager (the other one, who was not a complete idiot), I of course, was rootling about like a truffle-hunting pig under my desk with my backside facing towards him. Once again, I didn't detect his presence from the slightly unnatural hush in the office. After exclaiming loudly, "I've found it", and backing out in an unladylike and red-faced manner, only to peer up at his exasperated face, he looked at me as if he was thinking, "My God, this girl is a complete moron!"

I ended up going for an interview for another role, which makes me remember something else that in retrospect was sort of funny too. With so many of my well-meaning endeavours, they ended up backfiring or leaving me with egg on my face. I suppose it is a legacy of all bullied people, that a way to avoid a beating is often to use humour to deflect it. (I recently heard Dawn French on the radio saying that in a similar situation as a "forces brat", forced to move schools often, as I was in early life, she had chosen to clown around and be the funny one to be accepted. Of course, this honed her skills into becoming the celebrated funny woman she is now.) While my efforts did not end up being an advantage in later life, I did enjoy making people laugh in those early days, before later experiences served to beat most of the joie de vivre and comic tendencies out of me. With the innocence of youth, I did take every opportunity to take advantage of any potentially funny situation; it just wasn't always to my best advantage.

I once feel sure I was not offered a job, when, after an interview that I thought had gone without a hitch, I virtually shot myself in the foot on the stairs on the way out. As my would-be employer had stumbled on the stairs in the process of showing me out, I quipped, "Be careful, I don't want your job... and unwisely added to that "Well not just yet". I don't think he was amused...

On another occasion, always having had a terrible sense of direction, when I was asked after completing the interview if I could remember the way out, after cheerfully asserting I could, I turned and confidently opened the door of the cupboard adjoining the interview room and walked in.

The day of my next interview having been set, I found I didn't really want to leave. But I felt it was time. It was, however, made harder as, possessing an awesome immune system, in the several years I had worked at the factory, I had never had so much as a single day off work due to illness. As a result, I was in a dilemma as to what I could call in sick for. I knew that no-one would believe that the bionic woman (me), could be off for a mere cold or headache for a day, and I would not demean my sex by pleading "women's problems", (I did actually suffer badly with these at the time, but I never wanted to give anyone, least of all my new boss, a man who I felt didn't really like me, any reason to undermine me any further.) So, after several sleepless nights, I determined that the only reason I might call in "sick" would be if I fell down the steep stairs at my cottage.

The day of the interview dawned, and I called in and left the message that I had tripped while descending my stairs and had twisted my ankle so badly that I needed to get it looked at.

It seemed to be believed, so the day after the interview, before setting off for work, I wrapped my ankle up tightly in a bandage and some tape from an old first aid kit and painfully hobbled into work in the most theatrical fashion I could muster.

At the usual breakfast break, keeping up the alibi, I limped slowly into the canteen room. There, I was mortified that the lovely "dinner ladies" were all so concerned for me; they helped me to a table and asked what they could bring to me, rather than stand in line as usual at the counter. To complete my humiliation, after I had been given the special waitress service by one of them hand-delivering my sausage bun to my table, another carefully helped me to the door and held it open for me once the break was over. So embarrassing! I felt such a fraud and hated myself for deceiving these good people, but what could I do but maintain the lie? Otherwise, I felt I would hurt them and make them angry with me after all their concern.

CHAPTER TWO

WHAT DOESN'T KILL YOU

As a Forces child, who had been carted around the world by my English parents from my birthplace in Singapore, to Libya, and then to Germany on a couple of different postings, before finally coming back "home" to England, it had made for a strange and difficult childhood, moving schools and countries, sometimes as often as every six months to a new home, school and often country.

Most people are affected significantly by our first role models, our parents, and I was heavily influenced my mother, a remarkable woman who had enjoyed various exciting careers, starting from an early age as a childhood prodigy concert pianist, when she was talent-spotted by the TV celebrity host, Hughie Green. She then decided to train as a nurse. After she got bored of that, she performed in Blackpool as a showgirl, where her figure, great legs, and confident, charismatic were put to good effect. She finally settled down and married my father who she had met in a bar after a show she had been performing in, and where allegedly he was such a regular, he had his own reserved seat. (Read into that what you will, but I never saw him drunk. However, it is a well-known fact that military people are often accomplished imbibers of copious amounts of alcohol. It's part of the macho culture, I guess.) My mother was a larger-than-life character, and like most mothers, fearless in her protective instincts. She was like a lioness protecting her cubs if she felt we were threatened; and she could be a scary, formidable woman to be reckoned with. She once told us of a time in Singapore, when she was threatened by a rioting mob surrounding her car with three small daughters in the backseat on the way to school. Recognising we were in danger of our lives, she managed to stand them down by having the presence of mind to wind down the car window and shout out the Chinese word for "freedom". The crowd parted and let us go on our way unharmed.

However, my father was a strict authoritarian, who did not really want children. In addition, if he were to be forced to face that inevitability, he had made it known that he wanted boys and not useless daughters. This was to be made perfectly clear when he told his three daughters that each time my mother fell pregnant, we were each to be named Robert James. Sadly, for him, as well as not being great for our self-esteem or feelings of worth, we felt bad that he had the disappointment of being saddled with three girls (of which I am the middle one).

My mother had a great maverick, tomboy wartime youth with two younger brothers in tow, roaming about climbing trees and riding any horse she came across. She also often told us that she would have preferred to have had boys, as they would have been much easier to deal with, just needing a sharp clip round the ear to keep them in line. She also repeatedly impressed on us that we should never, ever, be so stupid as to have any children and went on to assert that she herself would not have bothered, but for the fact that in her day contraception for women was yet to be made readily available, so she had had no choice in the matter.

We were "seen and not heard", as my father, a brilliant but also troubled man, had been shaped by a rather sad and neglected childhood. His parents had doted on his sister and had damaged him psychologically by telling him that he would have had a twin brother, if it were not for the fact that he had kicked him to death in the womb. He was also exceptionally talented, being able to sing, dance, act and ride well. Although, he and my mother had a stormy relationship, they had great fun in Singapore where they had some fantastic parties and laid on shows that they acted and sang and danced in. (A sort of *It Ain't Half Hot, Mum* mentality I suppose). They were regulars of the eclectically and appositely named Anopheles Inn (named after the malarial mosquito), where my father had gained fame by being able to persuade any Americans from the military or visiting diplomats (as they were also friendly with the American Ambassador), that he came from the same state as they hailed from, and so could adopt a Texan, Bronx or southern drawl at will. He did this as a sort of party game or challenge. He had been seconded (loaned) by the Royal Engineer Corps (REME to the medical or RAMC division in the region), primarily to tackle the malaria problem and to serve as advance party for each batch of incoming troops. He also had to identify poisonous snakes as part of his remit. He cleverly found a solution to the pandemic disease by having the villagers breed a tasty fish in the many ponds surrounding their dwellings. This type of carp, called Eco Japonica, had as their favourite diet, none other than the mosquito nymphs or larvae that bred in these water sources, so they provided a bonus food source as well as having the beneficial side effect of drastically reducing the cause of a killer disease. Why he never got any recognition for this is still a bit of a mystery to me, but he was not good at blowing his own trumpet. As is often unfairly the case, no doubt others were more than happy to take the credit for his brilliant works.

He had a strict Victorian-style regimen and, along with the perfect table manners well drilled into us from an early age, he pushed us extremely hard to try and ensure that we could be able to attend university in later years. It was a sad fact that, although he was smart enough to have gone himself, in his youth, you had had to pay, and his parents declined or were unable to help in that respect.

I recall him locking first my older sister and then, later, me in the study until we had learnt our multiplication tables by heart, only letting us out to be tested on a chosen one to his satisfaction. He did also have an unpredictable and terrible temper, and woe betide us if we crossed him. I remember on one occasion him towering in rage over my elder sister after a disagreement; he tried to force her to agree that if he said black was white, that it was indeed so. I think here began the makings of my character in that I was a painfully shy and nervous child, primarily from having to witness at close quarters my parents having frequent heated marital rows, allied to the intimidation and strict discipline meted out from my father. I was bullied constantly at school to boot. All of this imbued me with a strong sense of justice, some degree of resilience and a strong instinct to resist any such behaviour in later life, and to fight back instead. I had witnessed the bravery of my strong-willed and incredibly stubborn older sister; despite what was must have been the terrifying ordeal of being shouted at point blank range (during which my father seemed to be mistaking her for one of his soldiers on the parade ground, who had been found guilty of insubordination), she refused to kow-tow and agree with him, and was eventually sent to her room to "think it over". I would like to think I could have been that strong, but I have always been better at defending others, especially the underdogs, where I wade in without any thought as to the consequences. This has not usually served me well. Standing up to be counted, or putting one's head above the parapet, is likely to result in getting it shot off, so I did not ultimately come out the better for those moments when I ventured "where angels fear to tread".

CHAPTER THREE

SNAKES, CHAUVINISM & APARTHEID

Eventually, after several interview gaffes, I managed to secure a position as a Marketing Consultant and after a couple of years, I moved onto another interesting job selling and installing retail till systems throughout the UK. I enjoyed both jobs, and thought I was rather good at them, despite continually being plagued by the self-doubt and low self-confidence that dogged me wherever I went. However, after my husband had been made redundant for the second time, as I mentioned, he decided to take up the opportunity to run the mohair production plant in South Africa and I also felt I was ready for a new challenge.

Having advised my employer of my decision to leave in order to go with my husband to Africa, it was something of an afterthought when, thinking about what I might do once I was over there, I suggested to my boss that I could start a sister company doing the same thing in South Africa: marketing and installing till systems. Somewhat to my surprise, he agreed to finance this by paying me a small retainer salary and providing some demonstration equipment. These were subsequently shipped over from the UK loaded up inside a modest company car for me to get about in. Conveniently, they also drive on the left-hand side.

On my arrival in Port Elizabeth, I secured myself some rented office space and, with the arrival of my car, collected all my demonstration equipment. I threw myself into starting this IT business aimed at selling the EPOS (Electronic Point of Sale) system in the Eastern Cape of South Africa.

Having seen the poverty and conditions of the native population on my arrival, I wanted to try and help the "underdogs" in that country, and so employed locals as assistants whenever I could in order to give them some additional income.

Initially I paid a lovely Xhosa girl called Patricia (who was employed as receptionist and secretary in the next office), to assist me in my business. Being curious to understand her culture, I asked what her real name was as it seemed unlikely that her "white" name Patricia would have been her given native name. I discovered that like most of the local population, she had two names: her real one, and the name used to address her by the white employers. I presumed that this was the protocol because the white "masters" found it easier, or perhaps it had been another way of impressing their dominance over the native population. Perhaps the locals themselves thought it would make it easier to obtain employment, if they had a more familiar name, I am not sure which was of these was the truest.

Whatever the reason, I felt that it a little insulting to have to use her alias to address her, so at my insistence, she shared her given Xhosa name with me, but after trying extremely hard to get my tongue around the special click that was a part of it and typical of that "Mandela" dialect, I am a little ashamed to admit that I never did get the hang of how to pronounce it. Patricia was kind about it, and just laughed as I repeatedly tried until I finally gave up, and so we agreed by mutual consent in the end, that I should call her by her English name. I like to think she appreciated the sentiment and my kindness and respect in that I always was especially careful to treat her no differently to anyone else I met, whatever the colour of their skin. This was later rewarded by her loyalty to me when facing a dangerous situation in which she quite possibly saved my life.

The incident in question occurred one evening after I had asked her to stay late after her normal office hours to help me. I had invited several pharmacy owners who had businesses in Port Elizabeth to come to my office one evening after closing, to all see a demonstration of my EPOS system.

I asked Patricia if she would like to earn some extra cash by helping serve some refreshments and some sandwiches and cakes, which I had brought in for my guests. I figured they might appreciate something to eat and drink while I went through my demonstration and sales pitch. I also wanted to be able to conduct my demonstration unimpeded and be able to chat about their needs without popping out to make coffee or pass round the food. Patricia readily agreed to help me, and the presentation went well, even though I discovered that there were some huge obstacles in the way of my being able to conclude any sales in this sector. These required me to ask my parent company for help in augmenting and adapting some of the software to their special needs.

One of these requirements was peculiar to the way that they employed delivery "boys" on bikes to drop off the prescriptions at their customers' houses. As payment was typically taken at the same time, the delivery boys were given a float so they could give change. They therefore needed my system to be able to account for that, as well as some software changes to cater for some private health care insurance plans, as of course there was no NHS in South Africa.

Typically, after finishing her usual work for her main employer as receptionist at 5pm or 5.30pm, Patricia would have gone out to the main road, where mini-buses known as taxis, would pick up workers (more akin to a low-cost bus service run by the locals for the locals). However, on this occasion, it being after 9pm when my guests had left, the last "taxi" had been and gone. She was therefore faced with a hike of several miles on her own and in the dark. I would not think of letting her walk home when I could drop her off in my car, a modest Renault Clio that had previously belonged to one of the engineers at the UK company, before it was requisitioned to be sent over for me.

Like most of the local native population, Patricia lived on a township or "location", as they are called in the Eastern Cape. Her house, (if you could call it that), was, like most of the others back then, mainly cobbled together from bits of wood, plastic sheeting and corrugated iron. Some were little more than cardboard and polythene constructions. Nevertheless, as is often the case with people faced with the necessity to survive, many ingenious ways were found to make their homes habitable, including re-purposing re-cycled and discarded items into something useful. Some notoriously used less acceptable methods of surviving like "stealing" electricity from overhead lines.

One of these improvised endeavours I remember that always makes me laugh is as a humorous anecdote I heard about a warehouse operative employed at my husbands' mohair plant. This individual had the supremely inappropriate nickname of Wiseman, as sadly I think his intelligence was not considered to be his strongest suit. On the day in question, he had decided to save effort and time on his daily task of cleaning the warehouse floor, not with customary brush and dustpan, but with the borrowed office 'Henry' vacuum cleaner. He rather ingeniously, I thought (as indeed he must have done), tied it to his waist with a piece of string. However, his plan was to backfire in the true sense of the word as, at some point in the cleaning process he had failed to notice it had over-heated somewhat. The other people there realised this when he was dragging it, engulfed in flames, behind him.

A less funny recollection comes from soon after our arrival into Port Elizabeth. I was made acutely aware of the suspicion and attitude to the local populace when purchasing a fridge for our townhouse. I was initially mystified by the addition of a lock to the door of every model I looked at in the showroom. When I innocently asked the salesperson why that was the case, he looked at me a bit pityingly and said, "It's to stop the maid from stealing the food". I confess I didn't know what to say or to think at that point.

Like most white people, our townhouse was located within a gated community. I was again a bit shocked and surprised to note that, like all the similar complexes, it was surrounded with barbed wire or broken glass at the top of the perimeter walls and could only be accessed by a special gate-opening remote control device with an electronic code, to be pressed when still inside your car. This was an indication of the fear of the white population that they would be robbed or killed by the poor, hungry local population. I learned that some houses located in the activist hotbeds, such as in the wealthy city of Johannesburg, had special safe rooms constructed, so that, if an attack or burglary were detected by the homeowners, they could all retreat behind the steel shutters to await either for the arrival of the police, or for the threat to go away.

I was also shocked to hear that, if an intruder was detected within a householder's property boundary, it was perfectly legal to shoot them dead. It was said to be common practice that, if a homeowner shot an intruder after they had exited the property limit, in order to avoid any possibility of prosecution for murder or wrongful shooting, the body of the victim would be dragged back within the property perimeter before the police arrived. Many also had armed private protection agencies. (They tended to come as a package with the burglar alarms fitted in the houses as standard and called "Armed Response"). They would also follow the same procedure, which avoided unnecessary paperwork and having to answer any awkward questions.

Shortly after we had moved in, when invited over for a friendly cup of tea by one of our neighbours, I quizzed the retired schoolteacher about the violence and the fact that most South Africans had firearms. She beckoned me to follow her and led me to the doorway of her master bedroom. Once there, she pointed to a large bullet hole on the door jamb. Shocked, I asked how it had got there; she replied that it was not fighting off any intruder, but it had come about as her husband always kept a loaded revolver under his pillow. One day, when she had her two young grandchildren over to visit, as she was busying herself making some food in the kitchen, leaving the children to their own devices, she was startled to hear a gunshot ring out. Rushing to where the sound had come from and noticing the absence of the two children who had wandered off exploring, she had discovered that the bored and curious little boy had found the gun under the pillow. He had pointed it at his little sister, who was watching and standing by the door. In a playful cowboy" bang-bang, you're dead" fashion, the shot whistled past the girl's head, narrowly missing her and embedding itself into the door frame.

This should have been another lesson for this green foreigner to take heed of, but I still did not really take it on-board, instead thinking it was all some sort of hysteria of the white population and did not really mean that I would be any danger.

There were tales of drivers getting out of their car to mend a puncture and reaching into the boot for their car jack and tyre, only to be shot with their own revolver, which would be handily sticking out of the back of their belt. People said that the locals were regularly searched and checked for concealed bags at supermarkets; one such chain was not referred to by their branded name – 'Pick & Buy, but was instead referred to, rather humorously I thought, as "Pick & Steal".

Although I had lived all over the world and in some dangerous places, I suppose, like most British people who spent most of their lives in the tame, law-abiding atmosphere enjoyed by the white middle classes in the UK, I had no real perception of what went on when the extremely poor are forced to rub shoulders with the comparatively extraordinarily rich. It is never a good situation, but I suppose I was naïve, and generally believed the best of the people I met.

Of course, I took some of the advice as being just common-sense when conducting yourself going out and about in any city or town in the world, but I generally thought that a lot of it was just the exaggerated and overblown perceptions of my fellow Caucasians. What finally succeeded in shaking my innocent faith in human nature was what happened next.

After dropping Patricia off at her dwelling, as I started to say good-bye and thank her for her help and prepared to set off back home, she stopped me and insisted that that she must wake up her neighbour to escort me down through the township, which was comprised of many hundreds of shacks, back down to the main road. Rather perplexed by this, I asked her why this was necessary and attempted to airily shrug off her concerns. My protestations of her being silly and that I would be fine, were over-ridden as she genuinely feared that I would be hi-jacked, robbed or worse if she let me go back unescorted. She pleaded with me, saying "It's not safe for you; your foreign number plate will be spotted, and someone will realise you are an outsider, so please let my friend come with you". Her wide eyes and deadly serious tone made a little shiver run down my back. Seeing that she was not to be dissuaded, she knocked on the door of her slightly bemused neighbour, who, once aroused from his slumbers emerged wearing only some long johns. He looked rather taken aback when he saw the white woman standing incongruously next to her car. (I was told later by my white compatriots that they would never be seen on a township location, as they would be fearful of stepping foot inside one, even in the daytime, let alone after dark). She spoke rapidly to him in Xhosa and, nodding in comprehension to her, he approached, and I meekly relented to opening the passenger door and allowing him to get in. After escorting me to safety back down through the location to the main road, he hopped out and set off to wend his way back to his bed.

On my journey home, reflecting on what had just happened; while I still stubbornly refused to simply take the word of what I thought to be the bigoted and prejudiced whites about the dangers from the local population, I did acknowledge reluctantly that it would be foolhardy to not take this salutary lesson on board regarding my own safety when it came from this kind-hearted, well-meaning local.

It therefore came to pass that I went on to hire Patricia's' boyfriend, a well-built, handsome Zulu chap, as my personal bodyguard, principally to protect my vehicle while I demonstrated my product, as he said that, in some places, it was likely that while it was out of sight, I would come back to find my tyres had been stolen. Also, after my rather humiliating experience struggling red-faced to pronounce her name, we just agreed that I could call him by his alias, which was the slightly humorous or perhaps ironic name of "Well-Done"; maybe he had been thus christened as a reflection of his mother's struggle in giving birth to such a strapping baby.

Once again, my naïve faith was once again a little shaken by something I discovered after hiring Well-Done who I had chosen after my positive experience with Patricia, in the belief that I was an excellent judge of character. I was therefore shocked to hear that, not only did Well-Done almost lose his job as a worker at my husbands' mohair spinning plant for having the stupidity to bring a banned firearm into work with him and stashing it in his locker, but also that he was a member of a Freedom Party, whose rather scary, inappropriate slogan was "One Farmer, One Bullet".

He also had bit of a reputation as being a bit of a Lothario (although again this sadly typified many of the males in the local population). It was more than likely he was unfaithful to Patricia; despite the developing Aids epidemic these superstitious macho men either declined to wear condoms or could not afford the luxury. It did also seem to be true that many of them also spent most of their own wages and their partner's hard-won cash, in the many native watering holes or "shebeens", as they were referred to by the locals.

I only found this information out after hiring him, but after the scary situation I had encountered at the location I admitted that I did still need a bodyguard. Sadly, this poverty and violence were still everyday life in the region and while I had been resisting it in typically stiff-upper-lipped British fashion, I recognised that even if I was not attacked personally, the loss of my equipment, or car tyres, leaving me stranded in the middle of nowhere would not be a great idea. Also, the huge EPOS till that was part of the equipment I needed to demonstrate, weighed in at around 1CWT (akin to a large sack of corn). This had the unfortunate consequence that, after years of humping it in and out of the boot of my car while installing and training on the product in the UK, allied to my stubborn streak in refusing to accept any help from mainly chauvinistic males I encountered, I had ended up with a lasting weakness in my lower back. This had the tendency to lock up and render me incapacitated if I was not careful when lifting heavy or awkward weights. Consequently, I thought he could at least carry my equipment in for me before retiring outside to commence car bodyguard duties. And I consoled myself that he would be company on the drive there and back and, at the same time, I could learn more about the culture and region.

Nevertheless, even with the bodyguard in tow, my husband's Afrikaner boss at the mohair plant once said to him, "Your wife must have balls of steel". Later, when we decided to rent a place a little out of town called Deer Park, his wife declared that she would "shit herself "if she had to live out there.

I recalled her warning in graphic detail some months after we had moved to this relatively remote area on the outskirts of Port Elizabeth. One morning, I was preparing to leave for the office. My husband had long gone off to the production plant (early doors as usual), and so as I left for work, having locked the inner door and padlocked the outer security metal gate behind me, I had walked halfway to my car parked outside when I was startled by a lone figure on a bicycle at the top of the drive looking at me. He was situated equidistantly between the "safety'" that was my front door and my car. My flight or fight instinct kicked in big time, as I realised that, if I was attacked, there was no-one to come to my aid. With my brain making the calculation in a few milliseconds, I saw that if he chose to make a run at me with ill intent, I could neither reach the door of my car to get in and lock it in time, nor could I run back to unlock the gate and get through the front door and safety. I tried to make it not look as if I was weighing this up. Instead, trying to keep a friendly tone in my voice, I said, "How can I help you?' The young man answered, "Do you have any garden work for me?" I felt bad that he had taken the trouble to cycle uphill on the steep drive which was about 200 yards from the main road to look for some work, but I didn't have anything to offer him; being English and not used to having "help", we did all our own gardening and housekeeping. I declined even to have the ubiquitous maid to clean for me as I somehow felt embarrassed to take someone on in that environment and did not want to be viewed the same as the other white "masters", as it was usual for the workers to call their employer's "boss".

It did not feel the same with Patricia and Well-Done, who I was happy to offer work to when I needed help and refused to allow them to call me boss instead of my first name. Also, despite having a full-time job, I felt it somehow wrong to have a maid come and clean for me; it seemed to me the relationship would never be equal under those terms. I had also been sickened by the attitudes of my peers to their domestics. I remember on one occasion, after desperately looking for what seemed to me to be a standard household item as prosaic and commonplace as a mop and squeezy bucket in every supermarket and hardware store and only finding a mop and normal bucket for my pains, I asked a neighbour why I could not find such a combo? After having to explain what I meant, to her obvious incomprehension of why one would need such a fancy contraption, I finally asked what her maid used. (The lady in question had obviously never mopped a floor in her life.) I was shocked to hear her say that they just used their hands to wring out the mop. I was at a loss for words, as I felt sure that with all the chemicals involved, bits of grit, possibly broken glass, and the unsanitary dirty water (I never saw any domestic wearing rubber gloves, as no doubt these were thought an unnecessary indulgence), it was a terrible indictment of their lack of consideration for their employees, who were not to be "spoiled" with anything to make their jobs easier.

All this advice came back to me with a vengeance though, when I was confronted by this unknown man at the top of my drive. I contemplated later what might have happened if he had had a hungry family to feed or the sort of bad character that the whites stereotyped the entire local population as. I realised that perhaps I was a rather stupid person to have allowed myself to be exposed in this way, but I could do nothing but try to put that thought behind me. I gathered myself together and said sadly that I had no work for him at the time; with that, he thanked me politely and turned his bicycle round and headed back down the track.

I could not decide that my attitude before then had been brave or foolhardy, but then as now, I hate to be bullied. My pride will not allow me to be forced to back down under any real or perceived threat, so I usually react in a knee-jerk and ill-advised way that, as I have mentioned, rarely turns out well for me.

I remember one such occasion, from which I did manage a lucky escape. It occurred soon after moving into the comparative wilds of the house in Deer Park, when I stubbornly faced off a hissing Puff Adder.

I had decided that a houseplant needed re-potting; I hate having to wait or delay carrying out any whim, due to a lack of patience. I abhor indecision in anyone, especially myself, and despise hypocrites. So, after many years in business, I had decided to live or die by my own dictum that, in the end, it rarely matters WHAT decision you come to, so long as you make - A decision. This can be another dangerous strategy to live by; many a time, I have regretted some of my decisions which I made too hastily and with little thought about the consequences. Even given several choices on a menu, I alight on something within seconds and decide what I am having, while other more relaxed bon viveur enjoy pondering the items at length and question the usually clueless and biased waiting staff as to what's best or what ingredients is are involved to the tiniest minutiae. It must make me impossible to live with.

So, having decided something needed doing, rather than getting into my car and find a garden centre where I could obtain some compost (and in my defence, I was not even sure where folks in Port Elizabeth went to obtain such materials), I had sallied down the hillside where I had spotted some nice rich loose soil. With the larger pot in hand, I proceeded to dig energetically away with my trowel to fill it with my booty, but then I heard a slight hissing sound emanating from close by. As I stubbornly continued to hack away, wanting to finish my mission and be gone before long, I noticed the hissing started to elevate in intensity and duration and concluded that it must be coming from the widely feared, deadly Puff Adder that frequented the area. I knew about them, as I had heard my father talk about them being one of the deadliest snakes known to man all those years ago when recounting his army experiences in Singapore and Malaya. I had undoubtedly annoyed her. (I assume that the snake must have been a "she", as most males when confronted with an annoyance that did not involve obtaining a mate or defending some food, would have simply slithered off to another spot to bask undisturbed.) I figured that I had come too close to her nest and having the temerity to start throwing soil about. Perhaps she had some live young inside the hole from which her angry warning issued. However, ignoring the threat, I stubbornly refused to be scared off and carried on digging until I had filled my flowerpot.

In truth, I was not afraid of snakes, even deadly ones like the Puff Adder. When we lived in Singapore, one of my father's special tasks was to become an expert in identifying and dealing with the venomous and harmless snakes in the region, so he could forewarn and forearm the incoming soldiers. As part of the job, he solicited the help of the locals to capture the snakes and then had the poisonous ones "milked" to extract the deadly venom by getting them to bite down on a piece of gauze covering a jar into which the pale liquid would trickle, this allowed the research and manufacture of anti-venoms, but also allowed my father to handle the snake as he did his presentation to each batch of troops.

Once, he recounted a memorable anecdote about when he grabbed hold of a cobra and starting his demonstration moving it from hand to hand as he started his talk to the assembled troops. However, he didn't notice the increasingly desperate cries from his assistant as he tried to attract his attention. What transpired later was that, due to some oversight, or miscommunication, the cobra had not actually been milked before his presentation that day; if my father had been bitten, he would very likely not have survived to tell the tale.

For us as small children, it was a common occurrence for us to come home from kindergarten and find some snake which had been recently captured; as they could not climb up the slippery sides, they were put in our bath for initial inspection before being transported to the military facility. My mother tells me we were even allowed to play with some of them.

Later, back in the UK, we acquired a pet python we named Charlie. My father, who was now a fully qualified probation officer having re-trained after retiring from the army and got a job as the Warden of a Hostel (for "naughty boys" we used to say) in North Wales. Charlie the python, was taken along and slept most of the day in the airing cupboard on the landing of my parent's house. He liked it there where it was warm, only coming out in the middle of the night to have a drink out of the toilet bowl or to indicate that he was hungry. Then the local pet shop had to be visited to procure a mouse for his dinner. I wasn't a fan of that, as I found it to be unbearably cruel, as the mice seemed to recognise the presence of a predator, even "British ones" who had never encountered a snake in their short lives. However, Charlie served as a useful threat and deterrent for the residents to desist from engaging in anti-social behaviour; most normal human beings have a fear of our reptilian friends. It is usually an unfair reputation; for instance, Rat Snakes are a real benefit in tropical climes; as their name suggests, they are useful in keeping these less than welcome rodents away from human residences. Nevertheless, some uneducated persons would be less than thrilled when discovering a "guest" in their woodpile, and so my father was repeatedly called out to capture and re-locate them as well as less beneficial varieties.

Unlike the two-legged variety on earth, I generally find that most animals are not motivated by any dark and sinister thoughts, only a desire to be left alone.

Another example of this is the Boomslang, a bird-eating, tree-dwelling and notoriously fatally poisonous south African snake. If bitten by one and not rushed to hospital in time, the result will be severe tissue breakdown and almost certain death. However, in fact they are extremely shy and tend to stay out of humans' way so are not one of the biggest man-killers. Conversely, the Puff Adder does have a much more significant reputation for causing more human deaths, as they like to sleep under or adjacent to logs, basking in the warmth of the day. So, if unwary feet should startle them from their slumbers, they react by delivering a backward striking and often fatal bite.

Annoyed as my adder undoubtedly was at my rootling around her burrow, I knew she was just trying to warn me off, so, without pushing my luck too far, as soon as my mission was completed, I did back away carefully and beat a hasty retreat to the house.

So despite these digressions, at that at this stage you might get an inkling that the warning bells of the attitudes and chauvinism I had started to encounter would make it difficult to pursue my own business goals in South Africa.

Proof positive of this was one incident when I managed to secure an appointment to demonstrate my till system at a remote hardware and grocery store. The store owner had been interested in having an electronic stock record and detailed trackable history of sales as he was convinced that items were being stolen or otherwise "going missing" due to some inside job or other trickery designed to cheat him. This was despite being set up like some Wild West film scenario, where the produce for sale was all kept behind a wire mesh screen and customers pointed out or asked for what they wanted. When these were totted up, they were paid for through a hatch, before the goods were passed across using the same route.

Having arranged the day to go across, accompanied by Well-Done riding shotgun so to speak (although, unlike most other whites over there, I was not armed), we finally pulled into the retailer's yard. I asked Well-Done to pick up the till and carry it in for me. I went through the door first so I could hold open the door for him and was met by the proprietor of the store, but as I advanced holding out my hand to make my introductions, to my disbelief and embarrassment, the owner looked past me to Well-Done. He greeted him as the would-be salesperson and business owner. This was a sickening moment for me, as, despite the racism of the Afrikaners toward the native population, he had obviously assumed, that, unbelievable as it might be to him, the black man would be the person owning the IT business, and he would be one who would be demonstrating the system. So, it must have been even more unlikely in his mind that this petite, blonde, white woman could possibly be that person.

I was very shaken and disturbed by this, and both mortified and discombobulated at having to set him straight, so the demo did not go well after that. I retreated, and on the long ride home began seriously thinking over my options. I felt that if this were to be the way it would go, that I would perhaps never make a go of the IT business I had such high hopes for given the chauvinistic attitudes that prevailed at that time.

It was made more difficult for me, as like most people entering a new environment or culture, I wanted to be accepted, and to make new friends to socialise with outside of work, and so I had been looking forward to attending my first '10 Beer Braai' (the South African name for BBQ). These were so called, as it was said the time it took to consume this many bottles of beer, was how long it took the coals to be just right to start cooking the large, assorted hunks of red meat. They might include Springbok, (a sort of antelope), or huge well aged beef steaks, that were usually served with chips (French fries). While waiting for the coals to cool in order to slow roast the meat, it was traditional to start with the traditional Boerewors' sausage, (derived from the Afrikaans words for beer and sausage) which was spicy and fatty, and usually served as a starter eaten with fingers and straight from the coals.

However, this also proved to be disappointing because at these ubiquitous get-togethers, the women huddled in an enclave discussing homely topics, while the men, in macho caveman style, stood guard over the fire, swigging copious quantities of the excellent locally brewed beer, and pontificating about sport, politics and business. I had no interest in children (having none of my own or any desire for the patter of expensive and time-consuming tiny feet to interfere with my career ambitions). I initially thought nothing of gravitating towards the guys' side of proceedings, little knowing that the disapproving looks, and cold shoulders cast from the other side of the divide would make me feel ostracised and unwelcome at future gatherings.

Meanwhile, as I struggled to launch the business, my husband busied himself with building production output at the mohair plant by obtaining new contacts and selling yarn to new clients all over the world. I once had the privilege of being able to watch him design a new black mohair yarn. He skilfully put it together using the expensive, difficult-to-dye kid mohair which was then mixed with small quantities of blue, red and green fibres to be combined into the most gorgeous, iridescent yarn which he hoped to sell to produce some high-class Japanese tailoring.

Despite his skill in the production and design of the various yarns and the fact that he had ostensibly been hired to oversee production, it came as a bit of a surprise to be informed, after he had been working there for a short while, to be told that that he needed to become more of a yarn salesperson. However, he was able to segue into this change of role without too much difficulty, as having experienced the second round of redundancy cuts at the production plants in the UK, he had had to transition from being the textile production expert to being a salesperson and had previously spent a while in the UK working as a freelance yarn agent.

His efforts working as an agent for another company based in the UK, which imported merino and other exotic yarns from Peru and South Africa, had initially taken him to the United States, selling yarn into a distribution company based there. His bosses were nice people, but he was only paid on commission, so as he was initially attempting to build up his customer and repeat order base, it was tough going, and slim pickings for us to live on. A while later, as we were having difficulty making ends meet, working solely with his Yorkshire yarn agency, I persuaded him (under some duress as he did not want to ask for "help" in any way), to ask for a retainer when he gained another textile importer and exporter principle working for a wonderful German gentleman and entrepreneur, who ran his business from offices in Cape Town and who lived in the exclusive, "millionaires' row" area of that wonderful city. He also had a quirky self-built beach house situated on the even more exclusive waterfront area of the city. (It was said that Mandela also had a property there.)

I had the privilege to meet him myself when, after we had moved to South Africa, we took a trip from PE to Cape Town, travelling the famous "Garden Route" for an appointment at his offices. We were also invited to have dinner at his main residence and to be introduced to his lovely wife (who I noted had also elected not to have "help" but had prepared the meal herself in their amazingly humble, old-fashioned kitchen). We were treated to a very fine, yet simple meal, but also had the good fortune to be able to listen to some of his amazing tales. He had a passion for sailing and had survived some crazy things. He told us about a time when he had been competing in a round-the-world yacht race. He was mid-way round and was in the lead when his rudder was broken by a passing whale and so commissioned a new one be flown out to replace it and continued the event. He was a character so fascinating that an entire book could be written about him. As soon as we met, I immediately liked and respected him very much. He made a big impression on me, as I was both humbled and pleased by his refreshingly non-chauvinistic attitude, so rare a quality over there. Not only did he worship his wife (and I felt sure he had never been unfaithful to her), but at one point during the meeting at his office, he leaned across and fixed me with his piercing blue eyes that seemed to miss nothing and said to my husband, "You should listen to your wife; she is a smart lady". I shall never forget that, as many times throughout my career, lesser men have not been able to look past my curly blonde hair and seemingly frivolous self-deprecating banter to see that I have a decent brain and can do a good job. I have a typically British, slightly eccentric, madcap sense of humour; but sadly, so often the outer casing that we inhabit irrevocably sets that all-important first impression, and this was the case with most people I met, both male and, more sadly, often females as well. They would judge me as being incapable of having any worthwhile opinions. I am sure I am not alone in this experience, but it was easy to feel insecure and to lose what little self-confidence I had in these circumstances.

Spurred on by his inspiring words and presence, and possessing a stubborn streak, I continued to dig deep and persevere at trying to make a go of the business, despite having diminishing assistance or encouragement from the parent company back in the UK. This made me feel very alone and out on a limb. Such was my commitment to trying to "fit in" and present a more suitable image of a serious businesswoman, I even dyed my blonde locks to a medium brown hue. However, despite my tenacity, and refusal to throw the towel in, it became increasingly obvious that things were not going well and that I might need a "Plan B".

Needing something to occupy my efforts, and worried that it looked as though, despite my initial high hopes and hard work, the IT business might not succeed, I started another venture in the shed at the back of my offices. I installed a designated power line and separate electricity meter and some other specialised equipment inside, all at my own expense, so I could work on an opportunity making some special waxing discs. These were used in the textile industry to help grease the yarn as it went through the spinning process. This helped minimise breakages that would temporarily halt production while the broken threads were meshed back together. I was desperately trying to find something that would allow me to stay in South Africa, as I certainly could not just sit at home doing nothing every day. Also, my pride wouldn't let me admit failing to make a go of it in this beautiful country for which we had both given up our previous lives to make a new home and livelihood. This situation was made all the worse by the refusal of my boss back in the UK to consider making the modifications that I had told him were needed to be able to market the product in South Africa. Little did I know at the time, but he had his own issues back home, as the new Windows iteration of the product, which was sorely in need of development if it was to stay competitive and remain a player in the UK retail market, was not going well.

It was then that the offer unexpectedly came from my boss to fly me home for a couple of weeks, ostensibly so I could help at a key exhibition in the UK. Feeling homesick and rather heartsick, I jumped at the chance (even though it entailed another fearful plane journey; I had a dislike of heights and had developed an intense phobia of flying). However, I was spurred on by the thought that I could see my parents and some friends while in the country again and I thought that that it would do me good to have a break from the round of disappointments and knock-backs over the previous 18 months. I also felt guilty that I had only succeeded in selling one system in that time and felt it was only fair to offer what help I could.

However, on my arrival back to the UK, I was rather surprised to be collected, not by some company employee at the airport, but by the owner and managing director himself.

Alarm bells sounded immediately; and it was soon apparent that my "recall" was not just so I could help at the show. Instead, the company needed me back in the UK to try and push forward the new product, which had been riven with setbacks and programming cul-de-sacs. My help was urgently needed to try and turn the product around as a key grocery retailer's contract was hanging in the balance. The very future of the business now depended on it being delivered without further delay.

I was faced with the reality of the imminent withdrawal of my funds and under threat of also having to return my car in South Africa (which had always been important to me as a symbol of independence). Even though I felt it was an admission of failure to come back to the UK and knew it would be difficult to leave my husband on his own, I thought I had little choice in the matter. Frankly, it was nice to be needed again. In fact, so great was the desire to bring me back, that I was able to basically name my salary, a choice of new company car (within a certain budget), a much sought-after private parking space directly outside the offices (these were like gold-dust), but also several paid for flights back to South Africa to see my husband. It was also supposed to be a temporary situation in which I would be free to return to South Africa once the software had been successfully rolled out, so it seemed a no-brainer to accept the offer.

It was a difficult conversation I had to have with my husband, and sad to have to wind up the businesses and arrange for all the equipment and company car to be shipped back home.

Although we remained married, I believe it almost broke the relationship; it was a trying time for us both, being separated by many thousands of miles and effectively living separate lives. However, on my return to England, I threw myself into the task in hand and eventually succeeded in bringing about the launch of the new software within three months of getting back to work. It was still not without its issues, and we still probably attempted the deployment too soon, but I got the job done, and began to make plans to return to South Africa. However, events then took a different turn, and, in the end, it was my husband who decided to come back to the UK. Once again, a new venture was needed.

CHAPTER FOUR

"NOT GORGONZOLA"

His decision to return to the UK was made in such a whirlwind, that it was left up to me to rapidly find somewhere for us to live just before Christmas, once he had wound things up in Port Elizabeth. I had been temporarily staying at his parents' house, but of course that was never a long-term option.

I remember bombarding various estate agents for anything suitable, but with little or no deposit to offer it was difficult as we needed a 100% mortgage to be arranged. When we had emigrated to South Africa, we had been forced to sell our first house at virtually what we had paid for it, as the market had plummeted just before our departure. We had managed to negotiate even this by including our hard-earned and carefully selected furniture, including a much-missed comfortable sofa and some Laura Ashley chairs. Regrettably, even to this day, we have never been able to replace them with anything as nice.

Under intense pressure to start up our life once again back in the UK, it was on Christmas Eve when I marched into an estate agent's office, where the sleepy and rather bemused staff had pretty much downed tools for the holiday period, thinking quite correctly that nobody in their right mind would be buying a house at that time. With tatty Christmas decorations that had obviously been up for at least a month, and some half-eaten mince pies, dotting the desks, they were startled to see me breeze in uttering the words, "I want to buy a house and I want to buy it now. What have you got to offer me?"

Unbelievably, as it turned out, they did have a house in a small village, which was not only at the ridiculously low price that we could afford with our limited budget and mortgage expectations, but also, fortuitously for us, empty and with no chain involved. Although this was sad for the previous owners, as it was a repossession, so this meant it could be purchased and moved into as soon as the deal had been struck. A viewing was arranged almost immediately, though I think it was the day after Boxing Day when I was shown round; despite its small size, lack of a much-wanted garden and only limited on-street parking, it had a lovely sunny yellow lounge with a real fireplace, and the ground floor living space opened out via some double doors to a dining area at the back of the house. This in turn looked out over some lovely views of open fields at the rear. Upstairs was bijou, in estate agents parlance. There was a bathroom, main bedroom, small spare room and a tiny box room that could hardly be classed as a bedroom, although a single bed could be squeezed under the window occupying pretty much the entire space. The kitchen was in the basement and the left-behind de-humidifier indicated that it had suffered some damp, but it was nicely fitted out and had the all-important back door where we could fit a cat flap for our treasured cats. We had had taken them with us to South Africa and planned at great expense to fly them back again, despite having to endure the mandatory six months quarantine before we could be reunited with them again. I therefore uttered the words, "This will do" at the end of the viewing; and after a brief conversation with my husband on the phone, with him unable to see it, he trusted my judgement and we went ahead.

Everyone will tell you that even a house that is empty with no chain involved cannot be bought in less than a few months, but by dint of a lot of pushing from me, and an excellent female conveyancing solicitor who I managed to secure the services of, all the searches, paperwork, finance etc. were completed in only four weeks and I was able to move in. Initially I was on my own, but I was joined some weeks later by my husband.

On his return he managed to secure an ongoing relationship as a yarn agent for our German contact and continued representing the Yorkshire/Swiss company he had worked for before the move to South Africa. This in turn meant that he needed to make more trips to Italy, Switzerland and South Africa, as well and significantly, building a strengthening business with a yarn distributor in the USA.

On one occasion he had been asked to represent the US company on their exhibition stand at the big annual textile expo that year in Paris. They would be launching some pashminas and mohair blankets based on the relationships my husband had built; these were manufactured in South Africa. As the exhibition was just across the channel for us, we decided to meet up with the Americans; and a few other spouses and significant others had also been invited to come along, so it sounded as if it could be fun and that I could go along for the ride as well.

The US principal and his wife came across, along with his key yarn salesperson. She, in turn, brought her slightly maverick boyfriend along who had a job of sorts, disc-jockeying at local radio station in North Carolina, and my husband who was interested in music of all genres and played the drums and guitar got along with him famously. The party was completed by another young American woman, who had had been brought on board to market the pashminas and blankets.

We all booked rooms at the same hotel in Paris. After long days on the stand, we were able to briefly decamp there to get dolled up for some great meals and raucous evenings out on the town.

The first of these evenings was terrific fun. It started with getting dressed up and, being given only about 20-30 minutes to get ready after returning to the hotel after the show, this left no time for a hair wash and blow dry. I had brought with me an auburn red wig cut in the shape of a smart bob which I had purchased some years earlier, so it seemed a great opportunity to enable a speedy quick change in the time allowed, and that it would be fun to wear it for the night out and serve as a bit of a talking point. The back story to this was that I had bought it after we had met someone in London with some friends. After a great party and the protracted pub crawl that followed, the evening had culminated with my husband (only fiancé at that time), eating Häagen-Dazs ice-cream out of the tub standing in the house kitchen, sharing it with a pretty girl called Karen. She was a housemate of our friends who had joined us on the night out. She sported a beautifully coiffured and professional bobbed hairstyle and I think he was a bit taken by her, especially as she had flirted with him outrageously all evening, demanding that he buy her a Kir Royale, at huge expense. Being young and unsophisticated, he had had to ask her what it was, before trotting off dutifully to the bar to procure it for her. (I am sure all of you may know what the drink is, but for the uninitiated, it's a champagne cocktail made with the addition of blackcurrant liqueur, turning it a rather decadent shade of purple). She had a highly paid job working for a well-known fashion designer and was used to being treated to expensive fare, so I suppose to her it was not much of a request. But for us northerners on significantly lower salaries, it was a fortune to spend on one drink at a price that would typically have covered the cost of a full round of beers and wines back home. I only became more of the "jealous-type" later, but at that time I was secure in our relationship, and so only teased him later about the evening, and although she was a brunette, whenever I wore the wig, I took her on as my alter ego – the thoroughly sensible and sophisticated "Karen". – This was a sort of homage and standing joke amongst our friends who were in on the story.

We had managed to end up with a bottle of champagne in our room, I think courtesy of the management, and managed to sup a couple of glasses as we got ready. Excited, and in a jolly mood preparing for the evening ahead, and already quite tipsy as the champagne was intoxicating on an empty stomach, I managed to make a speedy change into my evening outfit, complete with stockings (so I could utilise some of my nice matching lingerie ensembles) and some ankle breaking stilettoes. Then, with a quick make-up re-touch comprising some additional coats of mascara and a final slick of a bright coloured brand of lipstick, I completed the transformation by paraphrasing a catchphrase from our favourite Fast Show character of the time: "After only six hours in make-up, the ditsy blonde from Lancashire becomes the sophisticated London fashion designer – Karen". I did this while simultaneously pulling on the red bobbed wig.

We fell about laughing hysterically and giggled as we made our way down to the lobby for the "big reveal".

It went down a storm; it always caused something of a stir to see the complete transformation that just the addition of a different hairstyle can bring about. After much laughter accompanying a quick explanation, we trooped off en-masse to enjoy a superb meal, ending up with a customary cheeseboard for me, which I preferred over sugary desserts. I had requested my favourite Gorgonzola, but when it arrived, I ended up having a bit of an argument and some light-hearted banter with the waiter, as I insisted that he had not brought me gorgonzola, but some other (inferior), blue cheese substitute.

We finished the meal in high spirits, well fed, and not a little drunk, and while the rest of the party went to the front to pay the bill, I paid a visit to the ladies to refresh my makeup as we were going to move on to find some late-night bar to continue the evening in style. It was only then that I thought, wouldn't it be funny if I took off my wig and then re-emerged to innocently join our party, where our waiter would no doubt be hovering for his well-deserved and expected tip.

With more lipstick applied and the wig stuffed into my handbag, I sauntered up the stairs just everyone was about to depart. As I reached them, I wickedly turned to the waiter and wagged my finger at him with the words "' NOT Gorgonzola!"

It was a total coup de grace, as his jaw literally dropped as he looked at the person he had bantered with earlier as a chic, smart bobbed red head, now transformed to this crazy curly haired blonde. We were all able to enjoy the spectacle and witness his mind whirring as he tried to reconcile the two.

With peals of laughter ringing round from my delighted associates, I turned on my heel trying to keep a straight face and walked out the door but couldn't resist a backward glance through the glass door to look at the waiter's still bemused face as he stared after me, not quite comprehending what had just transpired. Just as I was just starting to feel guilty that he had been so dumbstruck by my little ruse, I was happy to see a slow smile of comprehension spread across his face, and then he laughed, pointing and wagging his finger at me in turn. I went on my way content that he had cottoned on and had no hard feelings for being the butt of my little joke.

It was to become a key memory and theme of the evening, as later the wig re-appeared at the bar where we had chosen to continue the evening. We drank many bottles, initially of good champagne, and then some inferior ones that I was convinced we were being sneakily served from under the bar, ideal to ply the silly, drunk and hence undiscerning tourists with. It is of course the truth that after a hideous amount of alcohol, it is extremely hard to tell a good bottle from a bad one (although I would like to say, that I thought I could still tell, having a good palate and "nose"). Finding it excessively fizzy and acidic (I usually prefer red wine over any white for this reason), I stopped drinking it relatively soon after the initial bottle had been polished off and replaced by some other brand, handily disguised in an ice bucket and wrapped in a white napkin. I noticed also, along with a fellow sceptic, that the smart Parisian "Madame" barkeeper, was careful to stop us trying to serve ourselves as she always snatched up the bottle if she saw an approaching hand, smiling winningly and coquettishly saying "Non, Non, I must serve you". I enjoyed her skill and artifice. It was only when the stupendously inflated bill arrived that it became a little less amusing.

I remember pictures being taken of the US owner with my wig plonked on top of his nearly bald head, then having red lipstick and other make-up applied in garish abandon accompanied by his not very convincing cries to desist. It was all in all, a totally fun night, only slightly marred by the eventual presentation of the truly extortionate bill for the champagne. While it caused a slight temporary dampener at the time, when we queried the amount, and the price was pointed out to us as being clearly published on a menu outside the bar. In the end, having little choice, it had to be split between two credit cards as it had exceeded the limit of our hosts, who had already paid for the meal in the restaurant. Notwithstanding that small downer, it was looked back on by all as being a truly memorable evening for many years to come.

Immediately following the Paris show, the plan was that the US principal and his key yarn agent were to extend their trip to Europe and wanted to visit the UK before flying home. The wives and partners had to return home due respectively to their family and separate business commitments, but the company president and his agent (who my husband knew well as he had worked closely with her while on sales trips to the United States and had stayed at her house on occasion) were both invited to stay with us at our tiny, modest home.

It also transpired that the new young female employee who had been assisting with the pashmina and throw launch, and who we had met for the first time at the exhibition, had also invited herself along. I thought this was a little odd at the time, and a tad inconvenient, as we did not have any room spare for her to sleep in.

Knowing something of our guests' spacious, well-appointed homes, it was nerve-wracking for me to think of what these wealthy Americans might make of our little terraced house, even though I was proud of what we had done with it, I felt that it would be a disappointing shock to our guests. Certainly, in the US company owners' case, he not only lived in a huge, beautiful main residence in a very exclusive part of the town where his business was located, but also had a fabulous holiday "log cabin" in the mountains. As the heir of a millionaire father, he was used to opulent living, to say the least.

To try and limit their expectations, I joked with them, while in Paris, that our house had rooms "the smallest size required by law", but it was also embarrassing to have to tell the pashmina girl (as I will call her, as she was also very well heeled, after her father had left her a not insignificant business concern), that we did not have room for her to stay as well. She didn't seem to understand, as she kept saying she didn't need much space, but in truth, with just our small spare room, which had an uncomfortable futon in it and the tiny box room, which we had reserved for our other two guests, we honestly had nowhere for her to sleep and, with only the one bathroom/toilet, it would have been a real problem. We finally looked up a local B&B and arranged for her to stay there, but it was awkward as after some enjoyable meals and nights at our house or local pubs in the area, we had to somehow manage to get her back to the B&B, when we had all drunk far too much to risk driving her.

Despite this minor inconvenience, we had some fun times at our house, where we had constructed a balcony with deck in order to house a chiminea and small BBQ out the back. As we could not afford to make a proper door to get out onto the deck from this first-floor level, the balcony had been built by my husband assisted by his father, not employing any professional builders; it was a make-shift affair and could only be accessed by stepping out through the window over the sill in an ungainly way, but maybe this added to its charm. It was nice to be able to sit out on the deck looking out on the night sky, chatting or just quietly drinking wine as we were beyond the glare of the horrid amber street lighting of the nearby towns of Bradford and Halifax and could appreciate the starry sky.

On another memorable night, our US guest had great fun; he said he had a long-held desire to "pour a pint" in an English pub, and the friendly landlord, happily granted his wish. On another day we also treated them to a crazy steam train ride with multiple stops involved at little stations where everyone got off and performed frenzied jigs in groups like demented Morris Dancers. Of course, everyone had taken plenty of booze for the journey as only the "Pie and Peas" catering was included in the ticket. I am not sure that mushy peas are a delicacy enjoyed by anyone but residents of the UK, but it was a novelty that added to the total and authentic Britishness of the occasion. At one point on the journey, which was a there and back affair, I remember dispatching my husband to grab a bottle of wine from our house which was about a mile from the stop where the train turned around. He requisitioned my ladies' bike, complete with basket at the front, in order to pedal back madly in time to re-join the fun before the train set off again.

Although we felt that there was not much to see or do around our sleepy village, we tried hard to make the stay as memorable as possible and put a lot of thought into the activities planned. Among the local sights we visited, was a trip to the iconic Bronte Parsonage, and also one of the stations we stopped at on the steam-engine trip was the one where Richard Gere famously had a scene in the film *Yanks*, as it was still 'olde worldey' enough to pass for a wartime station.

So, it was at the Paris show, and the days that followed on the extended trip to the UK, that the US relationship really tipped over from being merely a working arrangement between distributor and yarn agent, towards a friendship, which then resulted in the idea of launching a new business together.

These links forged by us were the beginning of what was later to become the trilogy of friends who started the successful enterprise in collaboration a few years later. We were undoubtedly the catalyst and glue that brought together the disparate worlds of South Africa and the USA, and it was through these key contacts established first as business acquaintances, and later as we were invited to stay at their respective homes in America and in Cape Town, that we were able to form the idea of going into business together and launching a new enterprise. All were to play their part so that the skills and strengths of each of the trilogy of friends could be brought together in launching our specialist running sock brand in the United States.

CHAPTER FIVE

TINKER, TAILOR, SOLDIER...

As I reflect on the course of events, I realise that our first mistake was believing that you can be friends with people you are in business with. At the time though, after many a glass of wine drunk over a convivial meal, we all agreed that what we wanted more than anything, was to be in business with great friends who had shared values and believed in having fun in their work at the same time as working hard. In contrast to our previous experiences in the UK, where it seemed that a "dog eat dog" attitude was all that was needed to get ahead, and that work was certainly not something to be enjoyed, we thought how fantastic it would be to put that Protestant work ethic behind us, while still working very hard to achieve our goals. We saw ourselves as being akin to the Three Musketeers, holding swords defiantly aloft, with the same "all for one, and one for all", declaration of loyalty and everlasting friendship.

Through the lens of what was to transpire, perhaps we should have been less naïve, and once you know the full story you can be forgiven for thinking what sad deluded fools we were, but at the time, after many grim years spent in the UK grafting (with me regularly putting in 50-70-hour weeks working for my employer), and through the horrors of my husband's redundancies, in which people less qualified than him were chosen to keep their jobs, it seemed a worthy goal.

There is a saying in business that the only good partner is a dead one, but although some little warning voices whispered in the back of my mind, we both had to put these thoughts to one side in order to forge ahead with building our dream unhindered by any doubts.

To attempt what we did, or indeed for anyone contemplating starting any new business, one must be totally single-minded, as it is a difficult and often bumpy journey ahead. It is not for the faint-hearted or semi-committed who may falter when the going gets tough.

We also felt it was an opportunity not to be missed, and that we would be cowardly and short-sighted to pass it up. It seemed that, if we never tried, we would always be left wondering "what if?"

In truth, while the honeymoon lasted, these initial plans, hopes and dreams at the beginning of the next chapter of our lives, made for happy and exciting times. We succeeded in pulling off the difficult (and some might have said impossible) feat of bringing together three nationalities and cultures in order to launch the new business. Looking back, it seems almost unbelievable that, in what was already supposed to be an over-saturated market, we succeeded in driving it forward from its inception to the $6 million concern it became in less than five years.

I have waited for over 12 years since the parting of the ways of the British contingent (me and my husband) from our erstwhile partners and friends, for fear of being accused of incurring any reputational damage to the business; but also such was the horror we experienced by the betrayal of these very friends and partners, that it is also only now that I feel able to bring myself to go through the pain of retelling it.

This first problem is now null and void, as a relatively short time after our departure and relinquishing of our shares, the business was subsequently sold (at I believe an enormous profit, by the remaining shareholders to a third party). They can now therefore be considered separated by the new ownership and the elapsed time meaning they cannot truly be affected adversely by any negative thoughts towards the company.

I have also deliberately not named the brand as a courtesy to the new owners and purveyors of the product, and in order to protect what was, and still is simply the provider of the best running socks in the world, whatever my personal feelings and sad memories about it. I still have some very battered and much washed pairs in my sock drawer as my preferred go-to, even though they always serve as a sad reminder of what happened, and the destruction of our dream.

As for our erstwhile partners and friends, I believe that they will now be either retired or are happily pursuing other avenues of their business and personal lives. No doubt, if they happen ever to read this book, they will recognise themselves and may not feel entirely happy about the way that they have been depicted; but it is the truth, and they can make their own peace with God and their consciences (if indeed they have any). It is also possible that some other people that were around those 12+ years ago may also know who our partners were, but I doubt that anyone will care what was done to us by them. As far as I know, the betrayal of friends is not yet considered a crime in any country of the world.

Here's a summary of the three elements that made up the partnership, (with due deference to John Le Carre's seminal work, from which I have re-purposed these nicknames in order to not directly name the parties involved): -

Tinker: This is the US yarn agent/distributor who had handy surplus office and warehouse space in a self-contained building and had existing distribution knowledge and contacts in the USA. He also had the money to invest to get the business launched (though little did we know that, in the end, it was financed entirely by the US banks. However, his contacts and existing relationship were certainly important in them backing the new business).

Tailor: The South African sock manufacturer (itself owned by a much larger German parent company) had the production capacity and design expertise to develop the new lines, and to "tailor" the brand and styles to suit the US end consumers. The husband and wife partners together ran the sock plant in Cape Town which had the specialist workforce who were able to make the difficult but then totally unique "seamless toe" which was one of the key USPs (unique selling propositions) of the socks. Instead of the usual method of knitting a sock "tube" and then machining the toe closure as an irritating lumpy line, (not noticeably an issue in day-to-day sock wearing, but imagine the tiny rub, rub along the top of runner's toes as they pound the tarmac, sidewalks or trails in pursuit of sport or exercise). This irritation can best be described by considering the adage that even a tiny but continual drip of water on the same spot will eventually wear away even the toughest granite. You can imagine the pain, blisters and eventually raw flesh that this seemingly insignificant bump causes when in the toe-seam of a sock worn by a runner. Runners we spoke to often reported that, to minimise this problem before they were able to use our brand, they turned their usual pairs inside out before putting them on for a run.

The "trick", based on the consummate skill of the South African workers was that they were trained to join the toe seam where the body of the sock is joined to the toe area through the very skilled and almost unbelievable feat of catching every single tiny end stitch loop using a special comb like instrument and then running a single thread through them both to bring about the almost invisible and virtually undetectable closure.

The second unique feature, which on initial telling sounds like a "so what?", as it seems an obvious way to make a sock when you consider that your foot is not a tube. While it is intrinsically roughly that shape from the toe back to the heel, and above that up the ankle, at the crucial heel area, which combined with the ball of the foot are the main points of impact in running or walking, a simple tube stretched over this part will cause the sock to move about and bunch inside the shoe. This rather fundamental consideration of the foot shape gave rise to the second key feature, which we referred to the "deep heel well". With additional shaping, extra yarn material was knitted into the heel area to allow for the extra volume needed and prevent it from creasing or riding up or down. While adding to the production costs and knitting complexity, this was another important ah-ha moment. When this was explained to runners and sports retailers in sometimes comical simplicity, the looks on their faces as they "got it" remain some of my fondest moments in the early launch and promotion of the brand.

As is the case with most works of genius or invention when looked at in hindsight, it might seem to be a rather obvious revelation and "not rocket science". It was of course later emulated by other manufacturers, but at the time it was pretty a revolutionary concept that somehow had been overlooked in most fundamental sock design. This may have been because other sock makers were ignorant of basic human anatomy, but it's likely it had more to do with the basic limitations of most of the typical commercial sock knitting machines, combined with the desire of the manufacturers to keep the yarn costs to the minimum.

Soldier: The third element of the trilogy of friends and business partners was provided by myself and my husband (the latter being the greater part as he had the expertise, the textile-knowledge, and the availability and ability to run the operation. He was one who acted as the primary matchmaker in the venture, bringing together the three elements to form the company.

I think that Soldier is a good name for our part in making it happen, as we were undoubtedly the troops on the ground, tactically making the roads and bridges to make "Operation BRAMSA". (This was not the brands name, but I will use it to denote the tri- nationalities involved namely BR(itain), AM(erica), SA (South Africa). It is also a name that my husband had used in his own yarn agency business in the preceding years, so it seemed appropriate to abbreviate the elements making up the partnership.

Despite being married to him, I was initially rather brought along for the ride, as I was not officially allowed to engage in gainful employment in the America. However, while modesty does not permit me to dwell too much on the contribution I made to what became a massively successful enterprise, I do remain very proud of the part I played in the launch and ultimate success of the business.

It is undeniable that the two of us, after bringing together the disparate parties to the table, did pretty much everything in operational terms, setting up the business and both office and warehousing systems.

My husband was a good choice as Chief Operating Officer or COO; having worked previously as a warehouse manager in the UK, he was also exceptionally good at organising people and leading a team. Having set up his own business before and being excellent with figures, he was able to work on spreadsheets, costings and to deal with legal and contractual matters at the same time. Allied to that he was adept at practical skills and, as he was also physically strong, he did most of the heavy lifting, even bolting together the racking units and constructing the conveyor belt system. Perhaps it's also significant that he was available and willing to uproot his life and relocate to another country, something that not everyone is willing or to do or will have the support of their spouse and family.

Meanwhile, on the office and administration side, I handled the accounting, CRM (Customer Relationship Management) database and even specified and modified the telephony systems to fit our purposes using my IT and customer service knowledge. I also set up the picking and despatch mechanisms, which were all under my control and basic design. I also had many years of marketing and sales experience to offer, which proved to be useful. Despite generally using the South African partner's expertise, I was able to proofread marketing materials, and I like to think that I also offered some other ideas and input throughout the brand's inception and growth.

However, my experience in launching my own businesses and somewhat eclectic knowledge gleaned from my maverick youth and army upbringing in various countries mainly went unnoticed and unacknowledged. I felt that, without a designated marketing role assigned to me, I did still contribute behind the scenes to the success of the business. An example of this was on one occasion when we were approached by a friend of the US partner with an idea for some cooling packs intended to be applied to runners' knees when injured or inflamed. On discovering that the main constituent contained in the packs was liquid ammonium nitrate, I recollected that this was not only used in some fertilisers, but that it also was a component in the manufacture of explosive materials. I quickly cautioned against the business investing in the idea as it would inevitably cause issues transporting the packs for us, especially in the USA where, after 9/11, the sensitivity to transporting any such materials, especially by air, would be a complete logistical and legal nightmare.

We did get some help in the early start-up stages, especially as the offices already had a basic existing phone system and warehouse area, and we had a few hours training on setting up the QuickBooks ledgers provided by our partner's accountancy firm. But the truth was that, in essence, we arrived in the country fresh off the plane, to be faced with a warehouse inside which there was a huge pile of cardboard boxes of socks that had been deposited in the middle of the floor, having arrived immediately prior to our arrival. Unbelievably, (even to me at the time), it took just a few weeks through dint of working around the clock to get everything up and running as a distinct operational unit and to ship out our first order.

It is easy to gloss over this as an achievement, but without the hard work and input we brought as our contribution, the company would not have been born, nor would it have been able to rise to the heights of its success without us.

CHAPTER SIX

WHAT'S IN A NAME?

But I am jumping ahead a bit here. First, we need to consider that anyone who has started a new business (or even those who have not), will appreciate that the new brand must have a name, and hopefully a good one that says something about the product. It must also be memorable and not mean something rude or undesirable when translated into another language.

Marketing textbooks are littered with some laughable or cringe worthy examples of the latter, like the infamously named toothpaste brand which was to be named "Cue", which translated means some lady parts in another language. Even an experienced and well-known international brand like Electrolux, infamously came unstuck when attempting to launch their vacuum cleaner brand into the states, as they chose to re-use their slogan 'Electrolux – it really sucks'. This was seen as a compelling slogan that had worked well in Europe, but of course it caused much derision among the bemused American housewives

More prosaically, and of key importance, is that any new brand attempting to enter a new market must not have a name that is the same or similar to another registered, trademarked brand that is already in existence. If it is, it could potentially be thought to be attempting to trade off that established brand's reputation or be confused with it. Ignore this at your peril or be prepared for some costly and potentially damaging litigation to ensue.

Launching a brand destined for sale in the USA is particularly fraught with complexity, as expensive trademark attorneys must be consulted to check out the proposed name for a new brand in all 52 states.

The brand that our company was to become went through at least three rounds of proposed names, each one failing the acid test due to one or more issues or conflicts with other brands. This need not be just in name; even the letter styling or font can cause the attorneys to start hyper-ventilating. Imagine the iconic K of Kellogg's, for example, or its chickens head logo, and you can gather that we had to be exceptionally careful. Any litigation, especially at an early stage in the brand's launch would be enough to break it financially, not to mention the fact that any documentation, marketing materials or, worse, identifiers woven into the socks themselves with the withdrawn brand name would have to be discarded and re-made, causing a lot of expense and delay.

We struggled to hit upon a suitable name for the brand; as the lengthy process dragged on, production of the socks and all packaging and promotional materials was at a standstill.

We once joked in desperation, that in the end it did not matter WHAT the brand was called, so long as it wasn't called "Shit Sox", but it did become an absolute nightmare to try and settle on a name.

I would like to think I helped contribute not so much to the final name that was eventually settled on, but in some of the thought processes that went into the choice. After struggling to get conventional names approved, but then having them all rejected as being too close to other brand names already in use, I suggested that if it's a native word, perhaps one only used in South Africa, we would be safe from any chance of it being the same or like any other brand name in circulation, and it could also be tied back to the socks manufacturing roots and heritage.

I suggested the Afrikaans word for sneakers, 'Takkies', but this was rejected as a bit too close to the slang word 'tacky', meaning of course something sub-standard or cheap.

At this time of deliberation and impasse, my husband was still living in South Africa, while I impatiently waited in the wings in the UK.

In desperation to finally come up with the name that was holding everything up, it was decided that he would have dinner in a Cape Town restaurant with the two South African joint partners, and that they would not be allowed to leave the table until a name had been finally decided upon, one which would hopefully finally pass all the trademark and copyright criteria.

After many courses and innumerable bottles of fabulous South African wine, a name for the brand was agreed upon, and an accompanying logo scratched on a paper serviette.

The name chosen was a Zulu word, meaning "to move quickly", and so it was that the brand was born; despite some last-minute naysayer's objections, we could finally move on with haste to launch the brand.

CHAPTER SEVEN

MAD DOGS AND ENGLISH

Our arrival in the US is rather a blur, as it was a whirlwind of finding a place to live, acquiring a car, a rather fabulous black Subaru Outback. (We found out later that it was the only car that all three Top Gear presenters agreed that they would be happy to own.) Even without that endorsement, I am still so enamoured with the model; I am now on my third iteration, though for car lovers, the diesel is rather a disappointment compared to the original agile, "goes round corners on rails", petrol version we had in America. Petrol or "gas" prices as they call them were comparatively cheap there, despite them complaining at every opportunity how much they had gone up; they clearly didn't know how fortunate they were.

Later I fulfilled a bit of a personal dream, when we bought a "British Racing Green" MX5 for my own personal use. I amazed the locals by driving with the top down, music blaring, heater on full blast, muffled up with natty fur hat in the depths of a North Carolina winter, when ice and snow were the usual fare.

This takes me back to when I took my first trip to South Africa in the middle of our UK winter. I was offered a free ticket to go across and decide if it might be somewhere that my husband and I wanted to re-locate to.

Having decided that it was imperative for me to check out what was to be our new home before taking the big step of relocating lock, stock and barrel, (including the three cats we had at the time) to another hemisphere,

I decided that I must take the trip. Annoyingly, I was forced to make the flight alone as my boss declined permission for more than one week taken as holiday, so my husband had been an advance party, arriving a week earlier to check out the country and city where the mohair plant was located and to consider the offer of employment on his own. It was a big decision, which was made worse for me, as it is a rather unfortunate fact that I truly loathe flying. Peculiar, I confess, for a person with a globe-trotting start, having been put on a plane every six months or so as an army brat.

Such is my phobia, that I now refuse to fly at all, even on the relatively short hop over to Europe, I always choose to take the train and put up with the added journey time and inconvenience entailed. At that time though, I could reluctantly be persuaded to mount the steps of a plane for an important reason such as this, but only if suitably inebriated by several G&Ts at the airport bar, followed by a few in flight Bloody Mary's, as a makeshift anaesthetic and source of 'Dutch Courage'. This would be topped off by few more glasses of wine with food, and maybe a brandy to finish off with. Like father, like daughter, I have always had an enormous capacity for alcohol and find it an excellent end of day treat and sedative to ensure a good night's rest. I feel sure I have regularly exceeded the recommended "units" in my years of enjoying a drink, but I have only ever been incapacitated once the day after.

I had visited my doctor in the UK to plead for something I could take to help with my anxiety, but he just told me to have a stiff drink and refused to prescribe any medication to help me cope with my phobia.

Later, a less strict doctor in the US, where they happily prescribe anything you ask for (or so it seemed in comparison), allowed me to be supplied with a nice big bottle of the anxiety drug Xanax. After that, I found that just half a tablet taken in the airport bar shortly before boarding, along with my pre-flight drink, rendered me nearly comatose for the scariest bit, taking off, and generally calmer throughout the ordeal. It also made it much less likely for me to grasp at the arm of any passenger who had the misfortune to be seated next to me.

Before having access to this wonder drug, I had been dependent on those airport and in-flight drinks to make the whole ordeal just about bearable, so I am sure had Xanax been prescribed back then, it would have been much better for my liver.

Indeed, harking back again to my honeymoon in Egypt, I was diagnosed with alcoholic poisoning by some friendly doctors I met after disembarking from the flight between Cairo and Luxor. On that occasion, before boarding, I had consumed a concoction of ¼ tonic to ¾ gin out of a surreptitiously filled water bottle. (This was before the post-9/11 precautions, but I was still not sure that alcohol in a mainly Muslim country would be tolerated, hence the subterfuge.)

As it happened it was probably just as well; after the plane got airborne, a brief announcement was made over the intercom in Arabic, which was closely followed by a congratulatory round of applause from the assorted local passengers. I could only deduce that this expression of praise and delight was intended to reward the pilot for having managed his first take-off without crashing. Hardly a winning endorsement for the nervous passenger. With all due respect, should I have plummeted to the earth for an ignominious death, I was hardly likely to be philosophical about having risked my life in some amateur's hands, even if it were deemed to be the will of Allah.

For those of you who ascribe to any fatalistic religion, I wish you all the best, but I had a lot of sympathy with my sister when she told me that, while working in Riyadh at a hospital where she was employed, she disliked having to be driven in Saudi Arabia. (Women were not allowed to drive themselves at that time). When I asked her why that was, she said simply that the Arabs didn't bother with having any insurance as any accident was deemed as being "God's Will".

Those of you who are happy sitting in an airborne tin can and have flown lots of times will probably be dismissive of people like me having this phobia, but I once sat on a train journey debating the various forms of travel with some insurance loss adjusters. While attempting to deprecate my own, as I saw it, irrational aversion to getting on a plane, I explained that it was not so much the sudden death that I feared, but the short yet terrifying plummet to earth after any incident or failure with the plane. To console myself I suggested that, after all, it would be only a few seconds of anguish if the worst were to happen. However, they told me (perhaps unkindly) that in fact it took several minutes for a plane to reach the ground even in free fall. They knew this because they had a formula to calculate the compensation paid out to relatives: so much for every second of fear the victims had had to endure before their eventual demise.

To set the scene for my arrival into South Africa, you may have gathered that I have always had a penchant for beautiful and dramatic stylish clothes, invariably topped off with a suitable hat to complete my ensemble.

Around that time, having recently acquired a full-length blue arctic fox coat (fake fur of course), and matched with yet another of my signature hats, this time an appropriately dramatic Russian number, (think Julie Christie in Dr Zhivago), I decided to wear it on the trip from cold draughty Manchester over to sunny Port Elizabeth in South Africa. Not only was it warm as toast but it also always drew attention, even in the UK, where we are not famed for batting an eyelid even when confronted by the extremes of London fashionistas. I think a streaker could run past Buckingham Palace, and only provoke any local bystanders to remark that perhaps it is a chilly time of year to choose to be without a vest. However, when I finally landed in South Africa and was greeted by the bright sunshine and heat of the African summer after the 11-hour flight from drizzly Manchester airport in the depths of our winter, my ensemble caused jaws to drop in obvious disbelief.

We had taxied across the tarmac to halt in front of the small terminus building at the tiny Port Elizabeth local airport. Incidentally, I had been warned that this airfield was notorious for having cross runway gusts, which often led to some aborted landings or fly pasts; apparently, after enduring a scary see-sawing approach, it was often followed by a sort of "what the heck, it's now or never" dumping down while the plane was still some feet off the tarmac, before slithering ungracefully to a halt. These landings allegedly occurred frequently, as the pilot on a tight schedule, not wanting to waste fuel, or simply not being keen to have another go if conditions were still not ideal to make a more conventional landing, elected to just land the aircraft in what was obviously a manner unlikely to impress their passengers. However, being armed with this unwanted additional information, only led to one or two more inflight beverages being consumed by me on that final leg of the journey.

Luckily, this landing proved to be uneventful; but consider the sight of a small personage, coated as perhaps Scott of the Antarctic might have been garbed, pausing unsteadily in the plane doorway, before carefully descending the steps, still slightly under the influence of residual Dutch Courage. Then, with hand luggage in hand, picture her teetering slowly across the small open space to the terminal building in high heeled thigh boots (also a favoured footwear choice at the time).

I suppose I must have presented quite a spectacle, even to my husband who was anxiously waiting to pick me up. He was usually tolerant and almost inured to my eccentricities, but the bemused check-in airport attendant at passport control gave such an open-mouthed look of amazement, that the devil in me just quipped, "I thought it might be snowing". It must truly have given weight to the "mad dogs and English" reputation, as I suppose not many people would have arrived in such bizarre and patently inappropriate clothing.

To his credit, after his initial open-mouthed shock, he just smiled, stamped my passport with a flourish and waved me through while shaking his head. (Probably thinking how dumb these English were to not know it's summer and that it never snows here, even in winter).

I hope he knew I was joking, although, when my husband stepped forward past some other people who were openly staring, he greeted me by saying sotto voce, "What were you thinking?". He should have known that I hate being cold nearly as much as flying, and leaving draughty Manchester in December wasn't going to have me dress for my destination, especially as a relatively short time later I would have to return to the icy blasts. Also, with only a week to pack for, putting my voluminous coat into my luggage would have left no room for anything else. I know people think I am either totally mad, or at best only eccentric, but underneath I do have some pragmatism and I find it a tad distressing that my decisions are so often second-guessed as being those that could only have been made by a "dumb blonde".

As you will have gathered, after a memorable week in Port Elizabeth my husband and I did decide to take the big step of relocating, but now let's return to our arrival some years later in North Carolina.

CHAPTER EIGHT

MOVING WITH SPEED

With the name of the brand safely secured, having passing trademark approval, manufacturing swung into high gear with the logo woven into the knit on each sock; style sheets for each sock variant could now be produced with packaging branded to suit.

In this phase there was frenzied activity on our part to ensure sizing matrices matched Europe and US norms and that we had sorted out various other important considerations on packaging issues, in addition to finalising the company setup and branding. Significantly, the partnership shareholding allocation and articles of association all needed to be written and finalised legally. All while we were still living in the UK as we prepared for our exodus.

This involved massive undertakings on our part sorting out our personal lives in preparation for our emigration, including putting our house up for sale, ensuring passports had been applied for, and ensuring my husband's work visa was all in order. This latter issue involved attending a stressful interview at the embassy in London, where permission needed to be granted for us both to live in the USA.

America is made up of a melting pot of nationalities and cultures arising from the many waves of immigrants looking to secure their place in the land of opportunity and so you may have thought that anyone, except for criminals, terrorists (and sadly, it might seem, Mexicans) would automatically be welcomed with open arms, and therefore that it would have been easy to be for us to granted permission to move and work there.

This was the case for some nationalities, as there were annual quotas assigned for each country based on population size. So, from less densely populated countries like Iceland or Norway with fewer applicants then the quota, entry could be relatively straightforward. However, for the UK, which has relatively large numbers wanting to settle in the land of the free, you must be sponsored (put forward by a US company asserting that the skills you possess cannot be sourced from a US citizen).

Luckily, the yarn chewing and years of experience manufacturing and selling yarns, made my husband's qualifications unique enough to be granted a work visa given that he was also being sponsored to work for the US company. This was not the case for me, so I had to be interviewed and only "allowed" to accompany him as his spouse on the understanding that I would not seek any paid employment.

It was a bitter pill to swallow for me; despite jokingly referring to myself as his 'chattel', I had run the till company single-handed in South Africa and had previously been employed variously as a marketing consultant, and then an IT trainer/ installation expert. I had even previously started my own business in the UK, the sadly abandoned- Baby-Grow Videos, so you can imagine that it was a little humiliating to have to say at the embassy in reply to the interview question, "So what will you do?" with the meek reply, "Keep house and write a recipe book".

Since I have mentioned Baby-Grow Videos, let me explain. It was a business I started in my early twenties. It began with a silent partner who provided two camcorders to use. It was built on what was quite a revolutionary premise at the time, which was to film around 30 minutes of key events of children growing up, from those first heart-warming shots of mother and father delightedly cradling their new-born baby at the hospital bedside, through memorable toddler birthday parties. The skill and business premise were to take this raw footage to a professional editing studio and create added value by condensing it to just 10 minutes of film cassette with suitable opening text titles and soundtrack music. I had acquired specialised franchise knowledge from consulting on two successful franchising business start-ups, and so my concept was to hire initially unskilled agents paid initially on a per event basis as the camcorders were easy to operate, and then as the venture achieved success and recognition to upscale it into a successful business model and then franchise it across the country. Some people at that time could afford their own camcorders, but in those early years of manufacture they cost around £1,000 each, and for those who did manage to buy one, the terrible, over-long wobbly amateur videos were a bit painful to watch back.

Also, as it was usually 'Dad' filming, he was never a part of the scene. My trained film takers did not have to be Steven Spielberg, if they took enough film of the event; typically, I allowed about 20-30 minutes maximum. Then I collected the film and took it to a professional editor I had sourced to make into a nice 10-minute snippet of these golden moments. Despite being well received by mother and baby groups, after months of hard slog and endeavour, I was forced to abandon the business, to my sorrow and lasting regret; I could no longer manage financially to continue as I was living off only my husband's income while I was trying to get my business off the ground. The heart-wrenching part is that I found out, just a week or two after dissolving the business, that I had been granted contracts to film in a local large maternity hospital, and after months of lobbying, had also been granted permission to film children's' birthday parties in McDonalds.

This experience did however teach me that a new business does need some financial input in order to have any chance of success; even with the best product in the world, it takes time to get things off the ground. So, when it came to launching our sock brand, we relied on a financial input from others, so that we could pay ourselves enough to survive until it took off.

Writing the cookbook was not just some random bare-faced lie to justify what I would do with myself after re-locating to America. It could have been the truth, as I had indeed started to compile a cookbook as a bit of a laugh. I ironically named it *Sluts' Suppers*. (My friends and family all knew that I was not the world's greatest chef). I also named it thus as it was yet another "feminine" skill, that I contrarily declined to try and excel at. According to my warped view of the world, it would have meant that my only ambition in life would be to make a good marriage and be a housewife and mother. (I also refused to learn to touch type at university lest I be used as a "mere secretary" by some chauvinistic male boss).

The premise of the book came out of a childhood with a restricted diet comprised of a limited repertoire of cheap and simple meals prepared by my mother (although in typical fashion, as with everything else she attempted, she was an accomplished cook). However, as she was forced to prepare meals for a family of five on a budget of just £10.00 per week, it left little room for fancy menus).

As an impoverished student subsisting only on my grant (awarded when my parents separated at a crucial point in my life), and later living on my own on a meagre starting salary, I followed in a similar vein. In these periods, faced with the necessity of surviving on these limited funds, for the 4 years of my degree, all week, every week, I lived off just one pound of fatty mince purchased at the lowest price I could find. I would start off by making a Bolognese sauce to eat with spaghetti. It was subsequently reheated each night masquerading as different meals by adding a few kidney beans and chili flakes and having it with rice, or a jacket potato. Thus, each resurrection was transmogrified into another meal. Eventually, bored with the constant round of meals using reheated mince, I would make up other "recipes", by culling ingredients found idling in my fridge or store cupboard that could be cobbled together into a something resembling a meal in less than 30 minutes. I would love to say that that other books published many years later on a similar premise by various acclaimed chefs had copied my idea, as indeed my jottings of some 20 recipes were compiled in an old lined exercise book from 1983 to around 1996, and pre-dated these later famous cookbooks, but sadly all of my scribblings were lost in the move back to the UK from Port Elizabeth and never saw public acclaim (or disdain).

However, despite the loss of the manuscript, I can still remember some of the names that that were intended to depict humorously the nature of the dish. "Fridge Bottom Fry-ups" and "Orgasm Trifle" come immediately to mind. This latter gloriously indulgent confection, the recipe of which was appropriated from my student days, had in fact already been christened before I re-baptised it for my own purposes, as 'I'd rather have Trifle'. The meaning may be clear as it came out of a group of my female student friends getting together at each other's digs, taking it in turns to cook something for the rest of the group. At the end of the meal, as I was not a dessert aficionado, I started the tradition where we would end with a cheeseboard of gargantuan proportions. This meant we could continue to sit round the table at the end of the meal, soaking up more bottles of cheap wine and sharing stories of the worst lovers or amorous experiences we had had the misfortune to have had. So, it was that after one of these torrid tales of disappointment involving inept lovers, we would often laughingly end with the words: – "Well… I'd rather have trifle'!

When it came to my turn, my contribution to hosting the meal was, of course, Spaghetti Bolognese, as not only was I not particularly good at cooking, but the antiquated electric cooker in my student flat had only one hotplate working, and that only had two settings, either off or on full. This was a tad limiting when it came to creating culinary wizardry, as even cooking up this simple repast meant the judicious juggling of the pasta pot and the saucepan filled with the meaty sauce back and forth onto the fiery red hotplate.

I can still remember how to prepare the decadent trifle, and it made it into the original draft of *Sluts' Suppers*, so maybe one day I will re-master the book along with all the other dishes, giving credit to the original creator any of those that were not from my own cobbled together meals.

Some of my more infamous inventions never made into the draft, being too bizarre for anyone but myself or the truly starving, to attempt to eat. An example of one of the rejected ones. I do urge you, even if apples, sardines and tomatoes are all you have left in your store cupboard, to never attempt to combine the three in the same pan (you will thank me for this warning). Another Sluts classic that I ate often, was the wryly christened "Pilchard Surprise", as it was greeted by cries of dismay one morning when one of my housemates opened the oven door to discover this concoction lurking there, left over from my dinner the previous night. I always made too much, but it meant I could avoid even the 30 minutes prep on some other nights and just re-heat it again, so not an oversight problem. This recipe was listed, ready for the fateful printing day that never came, and, despite its rather unappealing look, I found it a quick, tasty and nutritious supper, even before the health-giving properties of oily fish became a thing.

Sadly, *Sluts' Suppers* was never published along with my accompanying witty names and anecdotes, nor did the gastronomically inclined public, ever benefit from the way I described my recipes (or perhaps we can be grateful of this). In what I believe may then have been a ground-breaking approach, I carefully named the utensils required at the top of the ingredients list (as I found it so annoying to start making a meal from a recipe only to get part way through only to find that the "7" fluted flan tin" was not in my cupboard). Another device I used that was adopted later by some other recipe books was that I listed the ingredients along with possible helpful substitutes which "would do" if the item was not available. I also ensured that the ingredients were listed in the order that they needed to be added to the recipe, something I found very helpful as I like many amateur cooks, rarely did what we were told to do which was to always read the recipe twice before starting cooking. I still make the mistake of realising too late, that something that required some additional preparation before being added to the mix ended up being thrown in and of course then it is far too late to try and fish it out again.

Once again, I may well be accused of TMI here, and I do recognise my tendency to digress from the subject at hand. It is a recurring trait and probably a rather annoying habit. In various gatherings over the years, it has caused my husband and friends to roll their eyes in disbelief as once again, when asked to recount a simple set of procedures or anecdote, my butterfly mind (as my mother calls it) takes me off into some other realm and to seemingly irrelevant details, until I finally circle back to the point. Or, worse, I have asked, "Now, where was I?" in order to return to the point of the story.

Anyway, where was I? I was describing the process of going to America.

I recall as if it were yesterday, even though some 20 years have passed since that fateful US Embassy visit.

We had travelled down by train to London the evening before our appointment so we could get in line nice and early for this important appointment on which our plans to relocate and launch the business in America fundamentally depended. We had booked a modest hotel room and treated ourselves to a nice meal with lots of alcohol, perhaps due to a fit of nerves about what would happen if we didn't get those all-important stamps in our passports – a work visa for him and accompanying wifely chattel documents for me. We needed to provide an accompanying mug shot to go with the applications, and so we both got some photo booth pictures taken in the tube station the next morning, while en-route to the appointment.

I was gratified to see that my picture turned out rather well, despite the vast quantities of alcohol that had been imbibed the night before. You may have experienced this first-hand; sometimes, before the hangover properly kicks in, you wake up happily still drunk, gaily professing you feel simply fine, and looking in the mirror to verify this, you do indeed look remarkably fresh and bright eyed. However, as anyone who has had their passport or driving licence pictures taken in a similar photo booth will attest, this is not usually the case, (hungover or not), as you find that you end up looking like some police line-up of a suspected serial killer. I was therefore rather thrilled at the thought of being able to flash a rather nice picture at immigration for a change; but it was just typical of the bad luck that has seemed to haunt me, or perhaps the result of being such a wilful and indiscreet person, that my optimism was to be short-lived.

After waiting some five hours to be called forward on an unusually hot, humid summer's day in London (I believe temperatures soared to around 30 degrees Centigrade or around 90F), I presented my mug shot to the perky female jobs-worth official. There was no air-conditioning in the Embassy, and, as my hangover had properly kicked in, by that time I was looking and feeling rather the worse for wear.

After what seemed a cursory, dismissive glance, she infuriatingly proclaimed that my photo was not suitable' as she "couldn't see my eyes". I still think she was being unreasonable and bitchy. Looking at the photo I could discern, yes, two eyes, a nose and a mouth all present and correct, but I was unable to argue when faced with her intransigent cold stare. And I was in no position to protest, lest it jeopardise that all important stamp. I was dispatched to meekly go forthwith to some nearby high street chemist where I could get another one done quickly. At least she did assure us that we would not lose our place in the line once we returned with said photo as I feared we would otherwise miss our opportunity to gain access to our new life.

Trust me on this, and I still have the evidence somewhere to prove it: my ensuing facsimile made me look like some convicted murderer on death row. It was made worse by my sickly pallor and scraped back sweaty "rats-tails" hair. After waiting all that time, hungover in the stultifying heat, I wanted to make damned sure that she could see my eyes. As you might imagine by then I was feeling decidedly queasy, having had no food and drink for the preceding few hours' wait at the embassy. Nor could any hair of the dog could be risked lest we breathe alcoholic fumes on the "nice Americans" we were relying on to let us into their country.

Finally, after the truly awful picture was deemed suitable (I feel sure with a satisfied smirk, as the good one was ceremoniously binned by the snarky official), it was replaced by the "Cell Block H one", and I could wait in the next queue to go forward to "the interview".

After all the angst, and with my suitably adjusted humbler, tired housewife demeanour now much easier to fake, along with the "recipe book" story, I eventually passed muster and we were stamped and approved to gain entry to the land of the free.

CHAPTER NINE

BUILDING A BRAND – OUR WAY

As I mentioned, we arrived in the first week of October, to be greeted by a huge heap of boxes containing the initial shipment of socks plonked in the middle. It was no mean achievement that we shipped our first order, on the 17th or 21st of that month, if memory serves me right. That demonstrates the whirlwind of activity and hard work that we put in from the get-go, and that we truly hit the ground running, determined to get the brand off to a flying start.

Initially we did get a leg-up from our US partner, as we were able to utilise his UPS account for the initial shipments. And, until we got our own stock organised, we were able to borrow some cardboard boxes and packing tape to ship some initial orders. However, by dint of working 17-hour days, we quickly managed to get the accounting system installed, our own designated UPS account and equipment in place, and our own supply of assorted sizes of boxes the various orders. After that, we set up other logistics such as racking and a conveyor belt; before that we just had to pick the socks directly from boxes organised in style and size rows laid out on the floor and carry them individually to the loading bay for collection.

I handled the fax and telephone system and installed the database software I had brought with me, having had experience of using it in my previous roles. We were thus also able to quickly start entering our would-be customers details to keep track of who to contact, what samples had been sent out and other important customer service information. It was a multi-user version, so it allowed simultaneous real-time referencing by other users – notably my husband who, along with me, made the initial sales call contacts. You can gather from this, that I was not reclining on a chaise longue at home, sucking the end of my pen and concocting recipes for my book, but rather fronting up all the office and warehousing, order processing, invoicing, and as we had no other staff at that time, my husband and I shared the picking and packing of orders. Anyone happening to call into the warehouse would have been treated to the slightly bizarre sight of me trotting back and forth in my (inappropriate I know) high-heeled court shoes. Having been previously employed in professional and office roles, I did not at that time possess any "comfortable shoes": in fact, I did not own a solitary pair of trainers.

I had always felt I needed to dress professionally, in smart skirt suit and heels, even when required to install as well as train on the till systems in my previous role in the UK. I remember on one occasion; I snapped the heel off one shoe of a favourite pair of high heels while carrying the heavy till from my car into a large department store in Aberdeen. As I struggled with the heavy load from my car, which was temporarily parked on double yellow lines (which I had thought would be okay for unloading my equipment quickly), one heel became firmly wedged in a crack in the pavement. Unable to drop the till or risk the danger of straining my back even further by bending to place it temporarily down on the ground in order to extricate my heel, all I could do was to give a sharp yank to try and free it, only to hear it give a sickening cracking sound as it was broken off halfway up the shank. I was forced to hobble into the store in an ungainly and extremely comical way, like some demented Hop-Along Cassidy impersonator. With one foot elevated about two inches higher than the other for the rest of the day, I was forced to have to continue in the same vein, with my customer and his team, watching me struggling and limping around setting out my equipment and then while demonstrating it to the assembled store staff its features. There were some signs of sympathy and pity for my plight, but also some less kindly titters and jokes about the young 'Sassenach girl' as there was (and to an extent still is) a sort of competitive, anti-English sentiment inbuilt into the proud Scots. This of course made it especially humiliating when I wanted to impress them with my competence and professionalism.

Once again, this happened while I was trying to do the right thing, and to be perceived as a strong and independent, yet still feminine, woman. It was a sad fact that, in those times when women did jobs previously only done by men, they needed to pull them off without adopting the clothing or manner of the opposite sex. Those brave individuals who attempted to masquerade as "honorary" men, or to even "wear comfortable shoes" as the saying went, were called unflattering and derogatory names. As I've said, I was therefore determined to not ask for any help at that time, even carrying the very heavy equipment.

I recall one occasion, again when installing another of my till systems at a store; I arrived with my equipment (which I had loaded into the boot of my car unaided). I had been asked when arranging my visit to drive up to the loading bay for it to be offloaded. As I drew up, I spotted a couple of guys in the open-shuttered doorway having just unloaded another shipment of stock for the department store. After reversing up, I hopped out, went to the boot, opened it, and was about to heft the till out, when one of the chaps appeared by my side and leant down to lift it out himself. (Presuming perhaps that as a tiny woman in heels was about to carry it, it was insignificant in weight). As he took hold and attempted to elevate it, I noted his slightly startled look; he let go of it almost immediately and called out "Gary! Can you give me a hand with this?" The other man came down and, with both taking one side of the till, they proceeded to unload it for me. This having been taken out of my hands, literally, I just shrugged my shoulders, but could not help saying, "That's awfully kind of you, but I lifted it in on my own so could have managed". Ungrateful and churlish as this might have seemed, it was just the way it was then; but I accept my stubborn ego was my own worst enemy. My mother being from allegedly more even more male centric times, just accused me of being silly, and that men were chivalrously more than happy to help so I should just ask for assistance or stand back looking helpless waiting for someone to volunteer.

However, as the saying goes, these things make you stronger, so I was undaunted by any signs of derision from onlookers in the warehouse, having run the gauntlet of scorn from various quarters many times before. In the main I had survived it to earn their respect in the end, and frankly I was just too busy to waste any energy thinking about what other people thought. So, despite my inappropriate shoes, which also tended to get caught in cracks in the uneven warehouse floor and made a bizarre castanet click-clicking as I trotted quickly back and forth picking sock orders and taping boxes, we were off on what was to be a crazy five years building the brand in America.

The juggernaut continued to build, notwithstanding some pressures to change the formula for success we had so successfully set into motion. It seems simple looking back, but we researched listings of the branches of the specialty running chain along with the stores' telephone numbers; any other independent running and sports specialty outlets were added to the shared database. My husband and I then used to call each store, ask to speak to whoever was in charge and, after the usual sceptical reply – "We have socks" – we would give a brief description of the products and their unique USPs. Then we would just say, "Well you don't have to take our word for it; would you like a couple of free samples for you and your key staff to try them out for yourself?"

It was hard for the store owner or manager to argue with this or put up any objections to them being sent, so, after getting a few sizes and preferred thickness and running style (road or trail etc), the samples were carefully picked and despatched with the product sheets and price lists of all the styles.

The intention to call back a week or so later to check on how they had gone down was duly logged in the 'ACT!' CRM database. I had insisted on having this installed as an invaluable component of tracking the customers and prospects and noting what samples had been sent along with the key personnel's sock sizes and preferences and any other useful information.

As often as not, even before we had chance to pick up the phone again, we would get an excited call or simply an order faxed through to us. They loved the socks and so, when we despatched the first order, we were sure to include the genius concept of the free 'try-ons', where we took some of the slight seconds which had been put aside in the manufacturing process as having some small yet insignificant fault making them unsuitable for sale, and provided them free in every size, along with the range of styles ordered. This meant they could fit the running shoes along with our socks and, of course, not those of any competitor brand who didn't supply try-ons at all. It was so gratifying and yes, we made it seem easy. But as everyone who has ever cold called will appreciate that it's always a heart-pounding and stressful thing to do. We were acutely aware that, although we always asked, "Have you a few minutes to speak?", the busy and often harassed store owners could potentially have broken away from serving a customer. And no-one really likes being contacted by a salesperson they don't already have a relationship with.

Our philosophy was that counter to what so many of my bosses have said to me about the aggressive hard sell approach, and not taking no for an answer, you never "sell" anyone anything. Instead, you provide an opportunity to buy and then follow that up with excellent delivery and customer service. Sometimes it took more than one call to be able to speak with the decision maker. But I like to think that in those days, the unusual English accent at the end of the phone always took them slightly unawares and off their usual guard. It was initially an asset, and I like to think I also charmed them into listening rather than just slamming the phone down on yet another annoying unwanted sales caller.

Later, when I had built some rapport, I would also wow the caller when placing a repeat or new order with the "trick" of using the caller ID on the phone readout to quickly type in the first few digits of the number which gave us the area code. This meant I could answer the phone by saying the company name, my name and then quickly say "What's the weather like in [e.g.] Baltimore today, Bobby" using the customer's name from the database I had set up. Or I might simply have remembered as I have always had an excellent memory for names. It never failed to impress.

However, we were building a brand in a passionately patriotic country where, no matter how good the product you are selling is, the reality is that people buy people. This means that any prejudices or bigotry (which we all have), need to be circumvented and the "foreignness" of our accent could sometimes be an obstacle as well as an advantage.

When we entered the US running market, not only were there dozens of other companies already operating with a foothold in this relatively niche market within the scattered independent running retail arena (initially we deliberately decided to not try to crack the bigger sports chains), but there were literally thousands of other sock manufacturers. There was always the danger that retailers and consumers might believe that a sock is just a sock, and say," What's the big deal about one more?"

Trust me, we got that thrown back at us a lot; so, it was not a simple feat to change their minds, or, in sales parlance to "overcome their objections".

However, despite the "foreign" elements of the brand, and the English accents of the people selling it, the quality of both the product and the customer service were (even though as I say so myself) so impressive that, one by one, successive retailers were won over and brought on as new customers. Some of them even became ambassadors for the brand, as they would wax lyrical about them to others at any opportunity once they had been persuaded to try them.

The socks were so well designed for runners due to the construction of seamless toe and the deep well incorporated in the design, allowing the heel of the foot to be seated comfortably and preventing that annoying creep and bunching that typified most of our competitors' offerings. In addition, a variety of other features helped with the acceptance of the brand.

There were models made with varying heights, angle, low profile and the "ped" or "hidden" design where the sock came up to the shoe or sneaker line with just usually the addition of a nice, cushioned tab at the back of the foot to doubly protect the sensitive Achilles area and again prevent the sock from sliding down into the shoe.

We had varying thicknesses to suit whether a cushioned effect, or a thicker or thin style was preferred by the wearers and styles designed for road runners, trail running, and walking. (The latter was my favourite sock as it contained the magic mohair component.) Even after 12 years of almost constant weekend wearing, despite all that happened, they are still my go-to in my sock drawer.

The other "secret" ingredients, which cannot be divulged here in any detail, involved abandoning the totally unsuitable cotton fibre, which was bizarrely much vaunted and used in most sports socks at the time. You will appreciate this from trying to dry your bath towels; they do soak up moisture readily, but when wet will then hold on to it for dear life. With apologies for stating the obvious, you can then see that for a runner, sweaty or wet feet are a disastrous thing. We therefore spurned the use of cotton in our socks and instead a synthetic fibre was primarily used in most of the designs which had wicking properties designed to keep the foot dry. The use of nylon was also avoided; while it is strong and durable by nature, it can be sharp and can cut or abrade, especially if it is not well shielded from coming into direct contact with the relatively soft human flesh.

We also launched a range of cycling socks, but although these customers also found ours to be superior in quality to others, bikers seemed to purchase fewer pairs (perhaps because they did not take as much pounding), so these were less successful than the running socks.

On the most popular running models, we had the opposite problem to not selling as many as we would have wished. Instead, we became victims of our own success, as demand for these rapidly exceeded our warehouse stocks. This meant that I had to repeatedly plead for more of the share of production capacity at the plant (where they did not manufacture socks exclusively for us). This quickly became incredibly stressful, as our initially delighted retailers, who had been persuaded to purchase a few dozen in some initial styles, rapidly sold them and demanded more stock. This was exacerbated by our offer of free 'try-ons'. This meant that when fitting a runner with a pair of running shoes, the store assistant would be encouraged to say, "Hey, let me put one of these amazingly comfortable socks on with those so you can really get a perfect fit between sock and shoe". These try-ons also became a sought-after commodity as, once the sock was put on the customers feet, and they felt how gloriously comfortable they were, it was a comparatively easy sell on top of an expensive sneaker to add in a couple of pairs of socks with the sale. We also ensured, as far as we could, that the sales staff at the stores were trained in pointing out the features that made them so great. We heard tales about them waxing lyrical about the effect our socks had on their clientele; I remember one called them "Orgasm Socks", such were the ooh's and ahh's they received from everyone who tried a pair. We even discovered that one of our competitors' reps had been spotted wearing not their own brand of hosiery, but ours, which was a source of great satisfaction.

Demand grew so fast that I sometimes ended up getting pitiful calls and messages from our newly converted customers, as we began to consistently be in an out-of-stock situation and were forced to back order significant numbers while awaiting the arrival of more stock from South Africa. These initially patient customers would start to cut up a bit rough saying, quite rightly as they were cross, that we had persuaded them to stock these great socks, but what good was it when we could not continue to supply them. At this stage they had customers hankering after them and could not even tell them when they would have more of them back in store. We even got threats to stop stocking the line. While I did my best to appease them and try and get some action, there were several uncomfortable months when I was forced to "play God" and pick which customers would get the remaining pairs, even going so far as to divvy up the half dozen into single pairs to try and be fair with everyone as far as possible. That way everyone was sent something to keep their customers happy until more could be sent on. It also cost us a lot in additional shipping as I decided that it would add insult to injury to make the retailer pay for the back ordered shipments. Furthermore, even though some of the neighbouring states would get a normal next day delivery, California was typically five days' transit time unless we paid for more expensive expedited shipping; in some cases when a special running event or marathon was coming up, I would nonetheless take it upon myself to ship using the very high-cost Next Day delivery service, in order to ensure the retailer was not let down at these critical high value sale times.

Finally, it came to a bit of a head, when we were visited by the partners from Cape Town. I had saved one of the messages from a retailer almost in tears that we were letting them down.

This seemed to finally do the trick as they were able to experience at first hand, and not just hearsay from me, the fact that we would lose customers if we did not manage to secure a bigger share of production. Of course, that took a little time until the supply of socks managed to feed into the pipeline.

That wasn't the only issue I had to deal with. We had started off using the freight forwarder recommended by our US partner, but there were a few too many occasions when we were desperately awaiting the inbound shipment only for it to be held up at the 11th hour with a series of problems. Usually there didn't seem to me to be any valid excuse for the delayed shipment that I had customers anxiously waiting for and on which I had made promises based on the expected time of arrival. There was one particularly annoying incident when the forwarder was not only at fault, but, worse, didn't seem to care; I put this down to their cosy and seemingly unassailable relationship with the US partner. So, I looked for a replacement and fired the incumbent as soon as we had safely taken in the desperately awaited delivery.

This may have seemed been a bit drastic, as sometimes it really was just one of those things that happen that had delayed its onward journey to us, like maybe the X-Ray machine had broken down, or a batch had been pulled for additional customs inspection. However, I felt that it was just idleness or incompetence at the root of the problems and that they could do better. (Maybe I was harking back to my experiences at the lingerie manufacturer when we had been forced to tell some porkies about why a shipment would be delayed, but only after I had moved heaven and earth to try and meet the customer's expectation and as a last resort.)

In the end we went through three freight forwarders before eventually finding a trusted and reliable one from my husband's contacts based in the UK: but this was to be just one of the points of friction between us and the other partners.

It may be obvious to anyone looking in, but at the time was not evident to me, that whenever we hit any problems, rather than discuss options with our partners in the US and South Africa, we would just make decisions on the spot to resolve as we thought best. Unbeknown to me, and such were the egos and vested interests involved, that these decisions and the autonomous changes that followed, albeit made with the customers and business's best interests at heart, began to be a source of aggravation to our partners, and started the rumblings of dissent which eventually led to the betrayal and our undoing.

Another debacle was over something as prosaic as the question of who supplied the innumerable cardboard boxes of varying sizes we needed. Once again, I managed to cause a huge rift over this question of who we used. Initially we had again relied on the US partner's incumbent supplier, but we were always looking for a better deal. This became more pressing when we were having to make multiple shipments due to the back-order situation, and which was adding to our overhead in a significant manner.

We had had some discussions about moving from the less expensive plain cardboard to specially printed branded boxes, but again it seemed to be an unnecessary cost as the brand was becoming well known by word of mouth and I just couldn't see why we needed to pay the much higher price for the carboard boxes which would only be seen by the UPS drivers and at the store briefly before they were quickly ripped open to get at the contents. It just seems a pointless exercise in ego, so when a cocky, self-important sales rep who had been sent over unannounced by the US partner to secure our business for the printed boxes, swaggered unannounced into my office, I was irritated by the attitude, and hated being dictated to by others. It transpired that he was the owner of the box company, but did not endear himself to me by breezing in and not even taking any notes about what I was looking for. I did allow him to cross-quote though, as I was not churlish enough to behave unprofessionally. However, when the prices eventually came through, they were significantly higher than what I felt we needed to pay. It was not the box but the products inside that the retailers were looking at, so just could not see the benefit of paying the extra for the printed boxes as well as adding to the lead time if our demand fluctuated which it did of course. If we ran out of any sizes, we would be unable to ship or incur extra cost for having to use incorrect sizes of box as indeed dimension was a factor not just weight when shipping logistics are involved.

I thought our headed invoice that we placed in the box, along with a duplicate that I had organised to be used as delivery note, was a convenient and an efficient and money-saving device and would be enough at this early stage to reflect our corporate identity. But as a compromise, I obtained a nice large logo with our company brand and name, and as the rolls of delivery labels were supplied free of charge by the carrier, simply set it up so we could print these off in-house to be easily and quickly stickered to the outside of each box to identify the brand, placed next to the delivery label with shipping barcode.

As the costs of the shipping spiralled, I negotiated some great deals on some boxes that had been made surplus to requirement for other companies, and some of these did have the other company's labelling on, but by judicious use of the special brand label, this was easily over-stuck, so I deemed it "good enough" at the time.

There were no complaints except on the odd occasion when the delivery drivers had been a little too rough flinging the boxes about and this had caused some boxes to be damaged. However, as you can imagine the polythene wrapped half dozen packs of squishy socks did not need to be overly protected or gift wrapped.

However, this became another small demerit for me, as the disgruntled box supplier (a friend and golf buddy of the US shareholder) took little time in complaining that he had not got our business. However, once again I refused to be bullied or swayed. I thought that when we reached enough volumes we could look again at branded boxes, just not at that point.

Perhaps you can see a creeping pattern emerging and augurs of what was to come. However, if we had happy customers, and an increasing order book, we just continued doing things "our way" and everything seemed to be going fine.

CHAPTER TEN

SOX ON THE BEACH
& "JUST SOCKS"

The title of this chapter begins with a name of a cocktail we borrowed and re-purposed from the famous "Sex on the Beach" concoction. For the upcoming Running Sales Expo, we had, some might say, the crazy idea of having as an exhibition theme, rather than a dull 4 x 4 stand with a table, a couple of chairs and some samples and brochures on displays, we wanted to base it on a more attention-grabbing, fun theme.

Part of the inspiration was a mistake I made when researching sock competitors on the internet (as every brand manager must do as part of sussing out the market). I'm a terrible typist due to my stubborn refusal to learn lest I end up in secretarial roles. As it happens, I do confess a bit of a regret that I took this advice, which I was given at university, at face value; what I really should have done is learnt how to do it but kept it to myself. Not so smart really, as, after many years of wishing I could rattle off documents and emails at 100 words per minute, I am still doomed to a two- or three- fingers style along with the accompanying mistakes and incorrect auto-corrections I must back space and do over. Anyhow, I had heard of a big internet sock distributor called "Just Socks" and so happily went to my browser and typed in… well you guessed it, – it's not my fault that the S is close to the C on a keyboard, is it?

Maybe it was a Freudian slip, but whatever the reason, shall I say that I was a little shocked by what came up on screen. Then, for weeks after that, I was spammed with all sorts of, shall I say, "interesting and bizarre" links and images of proudly displayed male members – who knew?

When I recounted that anecdote, my friends back home just laughed and said, "Oh right, yeah, must have been a typo!" How very dare they impugn my good character...

But sex does sell, and our playful, quirky British sense of humour did creep into a lot of what we did. So, "Sox on the Beach" became a reality at the subsequent brilliant, and probably still talked about Running Expo Show stand.

The theme came from a brainstorming session, when throwing some ideas around for the show; we decided to make our stand a Tiki Bar complete with conical thatched roof, sand, and, of course cocktails (some of which were 'virgin' or without alcohol). Then there were the ones that, as designated barmaid, I described to the punters as being "with the special stuff" a la *League of Gentlemen.*

Once again, my versatile husband proceeded to burn the midnight oil constructing the Tiki Bar from planks of wood including a hand-made straw thatch unaided, hammering and nailing it together by himself in one corner of the warehouse for later deconstruction, shipping and re-assembly for the show.

When it came to the day, while the Tiki Bar was recognised immediately and enjoyed for what it was (though in my capacity as bartender, I declined to dress up in a hula-hula grass skirt as I thought it was taking the idea a step too far), not many of the healthy American runners and retailers had the foggiest idea of what "the special stuff" was when they came up and ordered their cocktail from the witty menu of drinks with the infamous "Sox on the Beach" placed prominently at the top of the list.

In retrospect, it was a bit silly of me to think that they would have even seen the cult British series from which I got this description of the illicit ingredient, but we literally had to smuggle the bottle of rum into the exhibition hall, past the eagle-eyed and no doubt disapproving exhibition officialdom and onto the stand. We had not gone to the extent of daring to ask for permission to serve alcoholic beverages, even though they were provided free of charge, for fear of being turned down. We knew some frowned on the idea of drinking hard liquor, even though diluted with various fruit juices and shaken with ice, especially some of the healthy athletes or purveyors of athletic merchandise. So, it was a way of trying to give a "wink" to anyone who might not be so puritanical. Consequently, when my question "Did they want their cocktail plain, or 'with the 'special stuff''", accompanied by what I thought to be a knowing look was met by blank looks, I usually had to surreptitiously raise the bottle of rum from behind the bar and show them what I meant.

It must be said that most took their drink duly adulterated, so proving that we were correct in offering it. If they declined, then all well and good, but this very British idea conceived by us, did come back to haunt us and to be used as an example of things not being done in quite the 'right' way.

The show, complete with the range of sock-based cocktail names was a great success. Many new customers were won over by the quality of the socks, and by the other idea of hiring a couple of masseurs to offer foot massages on the stand.

What better idea could you offer weary exhibition attendees who are already on their feet all day in their own retail establishments; or anyone who has trudged through any of these events knows that it is hard on the feet and there is little opportunity to sit down. So, we gave them an excuse to stop by to have a refreshing cocktail or to sit and have their weary feet massaged. This was so popular that we had queues (or "lines") and people coming back to our stand if they couldn't be fitted in immediately." Job done", I felt, whatever the nay-sayers thought.

CHAPTER ELEVEN

THE CHARITY – *MIRACULOUS FEET*

The rollicking ride that was the heady days of building the brand and customer base continued for a while yet, and we got involved with some exciting projects, most notable of which was starting a a charity to benefit a school for disadvantaged and disabled children in South Africa. The school was serendipitously based on the route of the famous "Comrades" ultra- marathon race. This was well known and revered by all runners as being one of the most gruelling races one could attempt.

We cannot take the credit for this initial idea as I believe it was put forward by the South African partners, one of whom had himself run the marathon and therefore had on-the-ground knowledge of the existence of the school and its involvement in the race.

The basic premise was to start a charity for the benefit of the school with the aim of raising enough money to buy a specially modified mini-bus with a disabled lift to donate to the school.

The children would line the route of part of the 90km Comrades ultra-marathon held annually between Durban & Pietermaritzburg and sell the beaded bracelets and necklaces they had made to the runners. These beaded items have now become familiar as having been appropriated in various guises as "friendship" bracelets, but this was back in the early 2000's, so it was quite a new idea. We appropriated this idea by asking the school to make more of these bracelets and some necklaces for us, to then be offered to the US running store retail outlets to sell on to their customers, with the proceeds going to the charity.

The idea was a wild success, though it did add to some of my logistical headaches. The first batches of bracelets were quickly snapped up by the retailers and after the subsequent generosity of the runners purchasing them when they heard about the story, meant we had to try and step up the production of the bracelets to satisfy the increasing demand and to once again to divvy up the supplies among all the supporters of this excellent cause, which had so caught the imagination of the stores and their customers.

Another offshoot idea came from my husband. As an amateur musician and passionate record collector, his somewhat ambitious and off-the-wall suggestion, was that as some great music came out of South Africa, we get together a compilation of these and make a record to be sold in the running stores, again for the benefit of the charity.

He wrote some of his own songs and had a full drum kit set up in our 'music basement' at our house along with some guitars, with which we had had the odd fun jams, so I suppose it was a slightly self-gratifying idea as well. But, in all honesty, who wouldn't want to be part of producing their own music record?

It was great fun getting the choice of music together, though rather complex as it was an unknown territory. We needed some expert advice and, of course, the production side was not something we were familiar with. But finally, the record was sent into production and the *Miraculous Feet* CD was born.

Not everyone can say that they have made an album, and although we can be accused of being a tad biased, we thought it was good. There was one track I would put on constant repeat as loud as I could on my short drive to work and home in my little sports car. It was so joyful; it never failed to lift my spirits and remind me what a great thing we had had a big part in instigating for such a fantastic cause. The start of the track has a genius moment where anyone who has been to Cape Town will recognise the whistle and shout of someone having a taxi hailed for them, which just added even more authenticity.

Admittedly, it was less successful in raising money for the charity, as it was a higher price than the few dollars paid for the bead bracelets and necklaces and hence not quite such an easy add on to the customers' sock and running shoe purchases at the counter. Possibly it was not quite to the American tastes, being neither rock 'n' roll, nor country and western, or any other of the mainstream popular sounds their ears were attuned to. However, I did manage to boost sales of the remaining CDs once the initial novelty purchases take-up had tailed off, by working hard on a promotional sock and CD pack. I designed and ordered some special boxes which could be made up to order with the requisite sock size and colour plus the addition of the CD as a nice gift combo. This culminated in us selling enough copies to justify the minimum pressing and eventually, along with the money from the bead purchases, this contributed to our final goal, when we could announce that we had raised enough money to purchase a specially modified bus for the disabled children, with money left over to build a special playground for the school as well.

I had to stay behind looking after the warehouse, while all the rest of the partners and shareholders were able to go to make the presentation at the school and be able to bask in the warm wave of satisfaction and pride as the children gathered round and sang in Afrikaans their "thank you" song. Later, I did get to see the photos and video of the day and to hear the singing. Even after all these years, it still brings a lump to my throat and tears to my eyes, just thinking about those happy, grateful faces, remembering their joyous voices, and what we had achieved together.

I hope that the school and the children were equally thrilled with their own achievements, as of course this miracle was also down to their hard work in producing the jewellery, and their part in the marathon from which the idea had sprung. Why do I say miracle? Well, it may surprise you to know that many of the children making the jewellery were either blind or partially sighted, so they had to make the beading by feel alone. A triumph over adversity by them and so richly deserved that they were able to have something in return to lighten their darkness and lives. The name of the charity when translated means "Light" or "Enlightenment"; we had titled the CD as – 'Miraculous Feet' due to the connection of this with the socks and running.

This remains one of the achievements in my life that I am most proud to have been a part of. Remembering it is made doubly sad since I cannot even play the record while in earshot of my husband, as the events that transpired soon after this crowning achievement, meant he cannot bear to be reminded or even talk of these times.

It may be totally wrong of me to try to make any comparison with troops returning from warzones who are unwilling to speak about their experiences, so forgive me for making the analogy, but what happened was so hurtful and crushing that, while it is extremely hard for me to write about what happened, I cannot even ask him to help fill in some small details, as it is just too painful for him to be forced to think about it. This is because he was wounded the most deeply and personally by the betrayal of his friends.

I have had to rely on my memory to pull back the events alone and unaided, so if I do happen to have some small chronology or details remembered slightly incorrectly, I trust that you will allow me that.

Notwithstanding any minor unwitting discrepancies, my story is a true and honest account of the rise and fall of our dream and it is my earnest wish that, once it is completed, I can try to finally look back, not in anger and regret, but with some sense of peace and acceptance.

I do not think I am there just yet.

CHAPTER TWELVE

WALKING THE WALK

The business was progressing in leaps and bounds and the initial bringing on board of a significant franchised chain of specialty running retailers helped open many doors. However, as you may know, every franchisee has a greater or lesser degree of autonomy when it comes to accepting or rejecting any "suggestions" made by the franchisor. (One of my previous jobs had been as a franchise consultant, so I was qualified to have opinions about this business methodology.)

In the case of McDonalds, KFC, Subway or The Body Shop, it is hard to imagine any of these would-be own business owners not wanting to, or being allowed to, for example, decline to sell a Big Mac or any of the other key products on which the original brand had been built. However, for some franchisees more autonomy is allowed in choosing to stock any product line and this was the case at that time with our deal with this running retail chain.

We did have the advantage of being given ready access and listings of contacts of these franchisees, which was to form a pivotal kick-start to our initial sales push, and we succeeded in most cases to persuade the sports retailers to stock our range. However, the consequence of this autonomy was that, despite this advantage, it was by no means a "done-deal" that every owner in this chain, comprising about 80 stores in all, would "roll-over" and agree to purchase even one style in our brand. We did also reach out to other totally independent stores, which was little harder as with no introduction to pave the way, we only had cold calling as a way of introducing ourselves. However, it did seem to me that we were doing well without needing any additional help.

However, our partners deemed it was not enough and so it was decided that we should employ a consultant who had been employed by the franchise chain. Indeed, he was very highly regarded in the industry and, as a runner himself, it did seem a logical step, as neither my husband or I could be considered athletes or to be able to talk knowledgably from first-hand experience about the trials and skills involved in running a marathon. My husband was a little sportier than I was as he had been part of a cross-country running team at school and enjoyed mountain and road biking from time to time. I had had an earlier encounter with the sport of archery, which I will describe shortly, but I was conscious that my general rejection of any form of exercise to date might count against me. Therefore, as I was potentially faced with someone who might doubt my commitment, or find me lacking in some respect, I started to go out running in order to improve my credibility and genuine knowledge of the sport from first-hand experience.

This meant that when my customers asked: "Do you run?" I would be able to truthfully answer "Not really, I have just started, but I am trying". I think this went down better than if I had been an accomplished runner already, as indeed their own livelihood depended on not only regulars of the sport buying from their stores, but also on newbies to the sport visiting their stores to be advised on and purchase their equipment, including running shoes, socks, shorts, vests and all the other paraphernalia needed to pursue it. Thereafter if they stuck with it, it was equally important that they return as repeat customers to replenish and add to their outfits and supplies.

For me it was mainly jogging to start with; as anyone who has ever started running will know it's a process, especially for those of a certain age. (I was 44 when I started). I was not particularly over-weight, but I was very unfit and possessed of a large D cup bust size; this had not been conducive to my earlier archery skills, as it interfered with the bow string on retraction. And even though I never suffered the pain of the infamous "jogger's nipple", as I never ran far enough or long enough to cause enough abrasion of that sensitive area, it was still extremely uncomfortable when running or jogging. Sometimes, when I awoke early and couldn't get back to sleep due to the cogs whirring in my brain, I ran to a nearby park while it was dark and still cool, extending my circuit slightly each time and staggering back. I also purchased a treadmill so that, on the hotter humid days, when I got home (usually around 6 or 7pm after shipping the orders, or even later some nights), I would pour myself and my partner a large well-deserved G&T. He was the better cook, so would prepare dinner, and I would take my "reward" upstairs, place it in the handy cup holder and do about 30 minutes walking on an incline and some running before going down to eat. I would also tell my customers I did this, as I figured it would be considered as just one of those crazy things the British do. However, in retrospect, I might have rethought this; sometime later when things all started to fall apart at the seams, this was just more "evidence" of our inappropriate behaviour when we were being painted as virtual alcoholics by the friends of Carlotta. (For the unfortunate few among you who have never had cause to see the most excellent Steve Martin spoof on Marlow – *Dead Men Don't Wear Plaid*, this reference will be lost, so I will briefly explain that they were the baddies of the piece who all colluded together.

As in everything I do, it was for the best of intentions; I genuinely wanted to show commitment and to be able to converse in a more knowledgeable way about its challenges and benefits, although of course running was not something I was really built for; I was certainly never likely to win any marathons. Even when a sales representative of the leading sports bra manufacturer kindly gave me some samples which made my running a less painful experience, it was not ever really something that I ever felt comfortable doing. The customers were always lovely and encouraging, and seemed to appreciate my attempts, as when I said that I had started running, they would always ask: "Are you enjoying it?" ... I was reluctantly forced to answer, "Not yet..." I hate to be disingenuous (maybe another mistake), so I am always honest, and I like to think people respect that. But then came the encouraging reply from my customers: "You will" ... In fact, I take a little morning jog down the prom every day now and, even after another 15 years, I cannot really say "enjoy" is the word. However, I like getting out in the fresh air and smelling the sea breeze and, as I battle the wind and rain, I try to not mind the ignominy of noticing that even pensioners and little children who pass by me, seem to be walking faster than I jog. I guess you need to get much fitter and faster for those famed endorphins that the runners always talked about to kick in.

My previous sporting experience aside from running came when I was forced to learn the skill of archery from scratch, when I had foolishly managed to get myself employed as an archery teacher at a Camp America in Connecticut. Once again, I had got myself into something that meant I had to make good on my word to maintain my integrity. The circumstances that led to this were that I allowed someone to "help" me with my application to work on a summer camp. I thought I would be employed as a counsellor (someone who is just there to keep a watchful eye on the kiddies), after which I could spend some free time exploring before flying back on the paid for return ticket. At that time, the prospect of flying to be able to experience this once-in-a-lifetime free holiday overcame my less severe dislike of flying. I hadn't yet developed the extreme phobia about flying that developed over time.

After completing my application form, my helper, the sponsor in charge of recruiting people and managing the process, noticed that I was not accomplished in any sport, but assured me that all I would have to do was to escort and keep an eye on the kids between their various activities. However, in order to show me in a better light and guarantee I would win a place, he had modified my application form to state that I had been awarded not just one, but three gold medals in Archery, even though I had never picked up a bow in my life!

As at the time I was knee deep in studying for my final exams, I thought little of it (though as always, I hate to lie about anything) I trusted his advice, and just thought to myself, "How hard can it be trolling kids around?" However, I was horrified a few weeks later to receive a conditional offer from the camp, which mentioned that "You may be required to take an archery certification test on arrival."

In a total panic but feeling I could not back out at this late stage, I discovered that I could take some lessons at the nearby university campus some 20 miles away, in order not to be discovered as a fraud. This involved the inconvenience of taking my old, battered boys' bike on a series of journeys, first to the train station, putting it into the baggage compartment, then hauling it out at the next station, to once again pedal some miles uphill to the university sports hall.

In the end, it was just as well that I took what might have been seen an unnecessary step, as I was informed on arrival to the camp, that indeed, I was to do the archery tuition for the entire camp. Also, it may surprise you to know, that after just a few lessons, I had succeeded in getting quite good (though not what could be classed as gold medal winning standard), and up to about the last week of my employment at the camp I successfully managed to teach several lessons a day. I nearly totally got away with it. But suffice it to say that I have never been so glad that I had the good sense, or just stubborn pride once again, to have taken those inconvenient lessons at the eleventh hour. However, I suffered for my unwitting deceit by being forced to give up precious revision hours to attend the weekly lessons while I was desperately studying for my final degree. Not only could I not spare the time, but also, weighing in at a puny 8 ½ stone at most (dropping nearly 7lbs or more by the end of the last exam, as I basically did not eat for the final weeks of intensive revision and exams), and possessing the muscle mass of a gerbil, I had been embarrassed that I could not even pull back the lightest 20lb bow at my first lesson, let alone have any chance of hitting any target. After that ignominy, I spent my days between each lesson, holding a textbook in my left hand, and with my "bow arm" or right arm, picking up a bar stool which I had borrowed from around our student kitchen table. Grasping it by one leg I held it with my arm painfully outstretched for as long as I could in order to strengthen my bicep sufficiently to be able to draw the bow at my lessons. It was also unfortunate that I discovered that, while right-handed archers would typically and handily be "right-eye dominant", meaning that you simply kept both eyes open and sighted the target easily with your right eye lined up with the sight, of course for me it was not to be that simple, as I was inconveniently declared "left-eye dominant". This was discovered along with my paltry bicep strength during that first lesson. This meant either drawing the bow back with my even weaker left arm or wearing a patch or closing my left eye to be able to accurately hit the target.

So, when I took up running, it was my first sporting experience in over 20 years.

The newly appointed member of staff was, as I said, a proper runner who had completed several marathons. He was offered a shareholding for joining the business at the level of our own small percentage. Initially, I thought he was a likeable and genial individual. I did have a few little nagging doubts though, even at that early stage, as he had come from the large running chain who had become our biggest customer. You may recall I mentioned that in my first job, my Managing Director had elected (sensibly in my view) not to put all our eggs in one M&S basket. I remember asking in my uncompromising and blunt way, if he was being paid any sort of retainer by them, (with the less than subtle implication that he could be a sort of mole), but he said this was not the case. Having said my piece, I just put the thought to one side, although I think others considered it rude and rather unwarranted for me to have even entertained such an unworthy thought. However, it did seem an obvious question that an astute businessperson might ask, and as always, no offense was meant by it. Nevertheless, it always seems it must be me that makes myself unpopular by asking the "Emperor's New Clothes question". Being an upfront and honest person, I expect everyone else to be the same. Though, if he had been paid anything by the franchisor, I suppose it was deemed none of my business, and indeed if it was the case, it might have been a pointless question as it is doubtful that anyone in that position would have answered in the affirmative.

In my experience, few people have the "cojones" to ask the difficult questions, or perhaps they just have the good sense not to, and just keep any such thoughts to themselves. However, having aired that and eliminated the tiny niggling doubt (at least for the time being), I moved on. After that, we generally got on well, and, other than the odd disagreement, as is usual in all workplaces, we came to look on him as a friend; he usually stayed over at our house in the weekdays when he came to the office as he lived a good few hours' commute away. He shared dinner with us on these evenings and sometimes a glass of wine, though he was not a big drinker, and we would all then watch a video, or some boxed sets of mainly British comedy shows, or *House* as we were fans, and that also reminded us of home.

It was also handy to have someone to occasionally cover for us looking after the office and warehouse, notably when we had to return to the UK.

We returned to the UK on three separate occasions in the five years we were living in the US. On two occasions this was to sadly attend funerals of two of my dear friends and once it was for a joyful wedding. The first return home was for the funeral of my first co-worker and French speaker at the lingerie manufacturing company, who I spoke of earlier, as sadly she had been diagnosed with a brain tumour that then proved to be fatal. This was after a series of radiation and chemotherapy treatments had ultimately failed to stay its inexorable progression. As one of my oldest and few remaining friends, she was forgiving and tolerant of my faults and was one of the rare people who could pull me up when I went too far. She was the voice of common sense and reason that I sometimes really need before I make any more of my ill-advised or stupid decisions and I still miss her friendship and counsel very much.

On a happier note, my oldest friend from my Business Studies course, finally decided to tie the knot. We were invited to what turned out to be an excellent shindig in Scotland where she lived at the time and still does; despite having lived in many amazing places, it remains my favourite country in the world.

Once again, for me to attempt these trips home, I needed to get either completely inebriated, such was my phobia of flying, or manage it with a combination of alcohol and my half tablet of Xanax, of which by then I had managed to get a supply prescribed, living as I did in the privately funded (by medical insurance) USA.

When returning home for my friend's wedding, it was just as well I had my medication, as, after landing in Atlanta on the first leg of the long trip home, we were held up, waiting for some bad weather to pass over, before eventually being cleared to take-off. We then flew directly into the wake of a massive thunderstorm. What ensued can only be described as a comedic version of an *Airplane* scene (though obviously not comedic for me or the other unfortunate passengers on this flight).

As soon as the flight attendants had been instructed to switch off the safety belt lights and had started to deploy the long-awaited drinks trolley, we hit the back end of the storm that had just passed over, and as the plane slammed into the choppy air, people were literally screaming in terror as the overhead lockers sprung open emptying their contents onto passengers' heads, and into the aisle. The abandoned drinks trolley, having only just been deployed at cruising altitude, was now crazily skating back and forth unfettered and unattended. You can imagine I was not too happy as, even suitably medicated, it was still terrifying.

This was just the start of a particularly gruelling journey, because, as we had been delayed in Atlanta, we then had to suffer being grounded for five hours on an unscheduled stopover in New England. Here again my much-needed alternative "anaesthetic" was unavailable due to some silly rules about not being licenced to serve alcoholic drinks on the ground. When we were finally allowed to take off again, now much delayed and panicking that we now wouldn't get to the wedding in time, I persuaded the air hostess to be unusually generous with the drinks trolley contents once we were in the air. As I remember, she smuggled us a free bottle of champagne as well, bless her heart.

After finally landing at Glasgow airport, having been travelling for some 12 hours or so, we had to run like maniacs through the airport, and then endure the interminable luggage collection. I was also awkwardly carrying as hand luggage a huge hat box containing yet another of my beloved wide brimmed creations. We were forced to anxiously await again for our hire car to be brought round for the subsequent ride of death at breakneck speed across to the Edinburgh side of the country. The car hire chappie shook his head when we said where we had to get to and for what time; in classic dour Scots fashion, like Frazer from *Dads Army*, he volunteered his discouraging opinion that: "You'll never make it."

But against all odds, we finally staggered into the venue where everyone was waiting, clad in all their wedding finery, in those final minutes before my dear friends were poised to say their vows.

Muttering muted apologies, I realised that, not only was I wearing my customary black blouse and stretchy trousers which I usually elected to travel in, but also that somewhere in all the turbulence, I had managed to slop one of the many Bloody Mary's ordered all down the back of one leg. But it was worth it as someone told the bride and groom, we had made it in the nick of time and the ceremony was able to go ahead beautifully.

I was thrilled we had managed to make it even with all the stress; by the time we were finally able to get to bed at around 5am the following morning, we were totally exhausted due to the gruelling experience and lack of sleep. I can honestly say having attended many weddings in my time, it was the best one I have ever been to… and that includes my own.

On my return to the office, things went on in the same busy vein and after a while, I reluctantly had to acknowledge that we were too busy for me to remain "the sole voice of the company" as I had in the heady start-up days, when I had answered the phone to all incoming enquiries. We therefore managed to hire a great receptionist to help, who was excellent, but then had fallen unexpectedly pregnant, so a replacement was needed. We also took on another individual to help with exhibitions. She was a young marathon runner and worked at one of our retail customer outlets, so she was hired to bring that first-hand, frontline experience to the business's growth. I was also released from the picking and packing of the sock shipments when we hired a warehouseman to look after this, such was the volume of orders coming in.

After advertising for a replacement receptionist, and trawling through a volume of truly awful resumes, some of whom felt it acceptable to send a CV without required covering letter, and others who thought that we would warm to their somewhat bizarre email handles, including such gems as fattygirl@ something.com. While we found this amusing, it didn't really speak well of a candidate to be the new front person of a specialty sports company. Most applications we received were also riddled with typos and spelling errors, so I almost despaired of finding anyone, but reluctantly was forced to offer the position to on an individual who seemed to have some relevant experience. However, my misgivings at settling for the "least bad" option were quickly realised as, on her very first day, when I was hovering, anxious to get her trained up on all the office procedures, she spent the morning on the phone speaking to her child's private tutor. While I had no children of my own, I respected that they were central to many mothers' lives. However, as I repeatedly popped my head round the door, indicating I was waiting for our training session to begin, it was to no avail, I did get very irritated as I thought a) it is your first day; and b) surely you could arrange to continue the call in your lunch hour. Then, when she finally finished her call there was no apology for having kept me waiting.

I made no bones about the fact that I thought it unacceptable but moved on to the training, thinking it was behind us and we could move on.

The next morning as I arrived at the office the new sales assistant sniggered a bit when I said 'Where's (name of new receptionist)?" She said, "You had better have a look on your desk". I went in and saw a white envelope on the keyboard addressed to me. Opening it I read a letter saying that she had quit as she could not work for someone like me.

When I shared this with the US partner, who called by later that day, and I told him what had happened, I was rather expecting to be backed up, having to my mind done nothing wrong. He just looked at me a tad accusingly and said, "Well what did you expect?" I was rather surprised at his cold attitude. And, as time went on, I felt that something had fundamentally changed from those happy collaborative early days and jolly evenings at each other's houses.

I did manage to find another replacement soon; when I was speaking with our hardworking loyal warehouseman, he mentioned that his wife was rather unhappy where she was working and asked if I would consider her. I didn't relish having another husband-and-wife team, as I knew from my own experience that it wasn't ideal due to holidays needing to be taken concurrently not to mention other occasions when I might would lose one or other of them or both. However, I quickly arranged an interview and was impressed with her and her work ethic.

She and her husband did not have much money and lived in a "double-wide" trailer, but they were lovely, hard-working people and only asked that, as part of their employment contract, on Wednesdays they could be allowed to leave early so they would not miss their Church meeting, which was held on that night. It was not always convenient, as often we needed to stay behind to pick and ship last minute orders, but I liked to be fair, and passionately believed then as I do now, in give and take in work relationships. I just decided that, if necessary, that I would pick and ship any last-minute ones that could not wait until the next day.

However, as with the other employee we had chosen, it seemed that the choices that my husband and I made independently of the other shareholders in our roles running the operations of the company, were not greeted with approval by the others. I was sad to have to acknowledge that both the new receptionist and her husband were looked down on by the US business partner for living in a trailer. I do not judge people on where they live, or how much money they have, and nor do I adhere to the myth that we British are all about class. So, it was yet another occasion when I found myself increasingly distressed and dismayed by the attitudes of people like him that clearly judged people in shockingly prejudiced ways.

I respected and liked them both very much and even after the "Betrayal" they remained loyal to us. This was a tribute to their decency and to how we had treated them. I really hope they managed to not be disposed of after we had left, as is often the case when a new broom seeks to sweep away all that remains of the old regime.

I am far from being the unreasonable person I was painted as after the summary departure of the first receptionist. It still rankles me to have been pilloried as such. At one point it was even said that I had "forced the first one to leave because she fell pregnant". This was patently nonsense. While I do admit to feeling a tad peeved and a bit disappointed when she announced she was pregnant and so would be leaving in due course to have the baby, and of course it was inconvenient to have to replace her, I still do not see how her leaving to have a baby and subsequently deciding to relocate due to a promotion opportunity that had been offered to her husband was anything to do with me.

But moves were afoot, and my unease was increasing, although I tried to stifle these feelings. I put them down to paranoia; maybe I should have paid a little more credence to my gut feelings, as they do not usually let me down. I am an intuitive person and can see the writing on the wall, usually way before anyone else suspects anything is amiss.

CHAPTER THIRTEEN

FRIENDS OF CARLOTTA

A new friend of Carlotta was soon also brought in who was another buddy of the US partner. Again, he was a genial chap, who I found amusing. I really liked his wife also, as not only were they a fun couple, but she also made a mean cocktail, something that is guaranteed to endear anyone to me. I make an excellent "Rocket Fuel Martini" myself' using 25 ml of very dry vermouth, plus 150 ml of very dry gin, shaken well over ice before pouring into a large martini glass with a sliver of lemon zest. I keep the vermouth and gin in the fridge so as not to have to dilute the drink with too much water from the melting ice cubes and to speed up the time between making it and enjoying that first decadent sip.

We had first met them both at a fun golf tournament in the US my husband and I were invited to, when I was still living in the UK, some years before the launch of the sock business. I arranged to come over from the UK in order to join the fun as my husband was already over there on a business trip which coincided with the annual tournament. This was part of the initial friendship reciprocation between us and the US partner. The new salesguys' house was handily situated next to one of the holes adjacent to the golf course, so it became the tradition for everyone to decamp there to have a frozen Mojito or two before moving on, suitably refreshed.

It was a great day and I felt I represented the English contingent well. I had lost some significant weight put on from my time spent in South Africa at the '10 Beer Braiis' and as it was also a tradition at my husband's mohair plant, for the managers to knock off early on a Friday and raid the beer fridge in the MD's office to have a few cold ones to welcome the start of the weekend, although previously never a beer drinker myself, I had also got into the habit of joining them. In addition to the pre-weekend refreshments, as it was so hot we got into the bad habit of drinking an icy cold beer from the fridge at home on most other days in the week. You will therefore not be surprised that, on my return to the UK after 18 months or so, I had piled on the weight so significantly that my parents had not initially recognised the hugely inflated person who presented herself to be collected at the airport as their previously tiny-framed daughter.

Realising that not only had my time in Africa not been good for my soul and morale, but that it had also not been beneficial for my health or looks, I embarked on a regime which consisted of, over the next three months of eating nothing but the cabbage soup diet. The diet, if you can stick to it, works not only because it is extremely low in calories, and the majority of what you do eat (how can I put this) doesn't stay with you for long, but also because when eating a diet containing virtually zero fat content, you cannot metabolise alcohol, so even a glass of wine made me feel quite unwell. This was helped by returning solo to the UK and not having the pressure of eating a proper meal with my husband, so I went down from a size 14-16 and around 11 and a half stone, to a size 8/US size 4, even fitting into a tiny size 6/US size 2 pair of jeans at one point. I maybe took it a bit too far as I had been a respectable size 12 and around 9 stone when I first arrived in Africa.

Anyhow, suitably slimmed down due to the stringent diet, and because living on my own after a long busy day at work, I just could not be bothered to even rustle up one of quick and easy *Sluts' Suppers* meals, I turned up at the golf tournament in a skin-tight "Emma Peel" black jumpsuit. Emphasising the Britishness, as no outfit was considered complete by me without the addition of a hat, I had also brought along a bowler hat, though I managed to leave it in a taxicab from the airport, which was perhaps just as well, as it might have been a bit too much.

So it was that, some years later, this the self-same salesperson, with whom I had enjoyed his wife's' mojitos, was hired by his friend and golf buddy because he had big contacts in the bigger "discount" retail sports chains, and it was thought that he would be able to bring some of these on board as customers.

While I had nothing against the new guy, both my husband and I thought that bringing him on with this goal in mind was a mistake, as we thought that having our quality socks appear alongside the lesser quality brands in these larger chainstore outlets would devalue the brand. We also knew that they would attempt to demand a big discount, being potentially big spenders, and so we argued that it just wasn't the thing to do with a premium brand like ours and we didn't need to discount it, however we were over-ruled, and the new salesman was hired.

I believe, in the end, he never did manage to sell to any of the big chains, and after a relatively short time, he moved on to another opportunity. I think we were saddled with the blame for that as well, as indeed we had argued quite heatedly about the discounting, and I knew that it had not gone down well at the time.

CHAPTER FOURTEEN

KEEP YOUR FRIENDS CLOSE....

I continued to work away behind the scenes and researched and found some suitable "Try-On" container bins to suggest to retailers; so they could conveniently hold the try-on socks in size order. I suggested a sort of hairdresser's trolley or bathroom cabinet style to the retailers with wheels and four or preferably five plastic drawers to house the sizes from XS to XL.

This was better than the single wicker basket most stores used as they previously wasted precious selling time rooting about in it order to dig out the suitable size, plus the plastic bins were a bit more hygienic, allowing the used socks to be set aside for the frequent washing which was needed. No-one particularly relishes trying on a sweaty sock which has previously been on various other peoples' feet. It also allowed the retailers to easily identify what sizes and styles they were running low on.

The subject of the try-ons was also to become a cause of a disagreement with the US shareholder. You can see that the try-ons had been like gold dust to us; they were always in huge demand as the range and brand grew, and, whenever we took any order, the retailers always finished off saying, 'Oh and some more try-ons please'. The top-ups were needed as, with the increasing demand for more and more runners to be fitted with their trainers including the socks, allied to the constant daily washing and drying, they eventually started to look a bit tatty. So, imagine my annoyance when rank was pulled at an open day; we were told to allow all the 'friends of Carlotta along with all their friends and families' free rein, not just the opportunity to buy some of the perfect stock direct (though this was also an issue in our low stock, hand to mouth days), but also to buy many of the precious try-on pairs at a cut-down price. I felt this very personally, as I had presided over them like a mother hen guards her chicks, to try and ensure our customers would have a continuous supply. So, I was incensed to see a load of them simply being requisitioned.

As time went on, the interference and increasingly didactic management and control continued. To my mind they were often trying to "fix something that wasn't broken". For instance, they suggested we hire a series of reps to go out to sell to the stores and to pay them 10% commission on every order, not only on any new ones placed or new account opened by them, but on any order, even if faxed in or called in by the store direct from customer accounts we had already opened and had regular business with. I was upset that, once again, our hard work in opening the accounts, building the order base and suggesting additional lines to broaden and increase the orders was just not thought "the way to do it". Instead, they wanted us to pay reps for doing nothing or for minimal or no effort.

The increasing need for control didn't stop there; I was forced to purchase and install a special PC server which was linked to our stock control system so the South Africans could dial in and "keep an eye on things". Again, not sure why, as we already sent regular reports on the sales and stock situation and being on the ground, were best placed to keep everyone appraised of what was happening and any trends in advance.

This worsening control situation was finally brought to a head when we were ordered to save and reserve stock for the franchised chain of retailers, who were our biggest customer, in order to service their needs over and above any other customers orders. I believe the fallout from this brought about the big move to oust us.

I understand the theory in business that you must look after the 80% and that perhaps this means giving preferential treatment. However, I argued tooth and nail that it was hard enough trying to look after all the customers with such high and increasing demand, which required an almost constant juggling act to try and satisfy everyone as it was. This principle (or to me lack thereof) was to become a big bone of contention.

Even if I thought, in hard-nosed business fashion, that we should leave other loyal customers hanging empty-handed so we could service any orders from the chain, this didn't sit well with my sense of fair play and principles. I also imagined the negative PR if this "favouritism" leaked out. Already, when we were running low on stock, the customers at the single independent stores often asked me whether it was because others were being allocated stock ahead of them. Some had even accused us directly of offering the franchise chain first dibs on the socks. I had always answered that we didn't do that, insisting (and it was a matter of honour for me) that we allocated stock as fairly or evenly as I could to all customers large and small as they were all equally important to us. I also argued that, logistically, how would we even "guarantee" the stocks for the "special" customers? Did we just try and guess what they might need using some previous (though hardly consistent) history of data, as the brand was still growing and, with new stores being opened all the time, it was almost impossible to predict demand. We had not, even by that time, exhausted the entire chain, as some die-hards resented the interference from their head office when it tried to dictate to them what lines and brands they should stock. I didn't blame them one bit, but I believed that they would be more likely to come around to us when they felt they were good and ready, although there was no telling when that might be, so again were we to reserve stock for that eventuality also? No-one likes to be told what to do, especially when running their own business, so I empathised with them.

Despite being the minor shareholders, I felt that it was our remit to run the business as we saw fit on the operational side, and, as my husband was COO, that he should be allowed to make the decision to change the way we worked. I reasoned that thus far we hadn't done a bad job.

It must be said that he was more amenable to making some of these concessions and perhaps I should have left him to discuss them and perhaps come to a compromise, but I was not backward in expressing my vehement objections to the idea.

It really did seem to signify that all was not well in our "happy partnership" and my feelings of unease and insecurity were only to worsen from that time onwards.

We also succeeded in incurring the displeasure of the female partner on the husband-and-wife South African side. She worked in the design and marketing side of the South African business and had decided that we should start stocking not just running socks, but also a range of garments including running vests, shorts and some other clothing in a variety of colours. These would need to be in many more sizes, and seasonal colours would be required as clothing was heavily influenced by Spring/Summer and Autumn/Winter fashion trends. From my husband's experience selling into the fashion manufacturers, and mine from working at the lingerie company, we knew that this was potentially a risky scenario.

We all attended a sales meeting in South Africa to have a look at the garments samples as she had, despite our initial misgivings, forged ahead with having some produced for us all to consider.

Admittedly they did look extremely nice, but we were not arguing that they didn't. We were simply saying that trying to control a massively increased range, with all the changes of colours and sizes required at least two if not four times a year, would not be a smart thing to get into and certainly not at the time when we were still building on the sock sales. In addition, they had added a sister company selling the specialist diabetic socks which was not doing nearly so well, being quite a small niche market.

I know that she was extremely disappointed to have the idea rejected and I think, at the time, we did have the backing of the US partner. However, he left it to us to be the nay-sayers, so we once again made ourselves unpopular with our partners by speaking our minds.

I remember we also rejected an idea which was the brainchild of the marathon running partner, which was to start designing and production of our own line of trainers.

Once again, his design looked fantastic and we knew it would be a good product; however, with the likes of Nike; New Balance, Brooks and Asics as our competition, and the costs of setting up production, again with all the massive number of size and width variants and seasonality of colours, it would be particularly challenging. However, the biggest issue was the many thousands of dollars that would be needed to set up the footbed machines or "lasts". He was forced to concede that it was something that, at that time we were not able to risk, and that we might not even secure the investment, as we had no existing manufacturing facility as we had with the socks.

At the time when all these events were happening, for the most part we just believed that we were doing our jobs running the company and, although we were open to new ideas, if we did not think that they would be beneficial to pursue them, we just were open and honest about why we were not in agreement.

Should we have made our objections and reasons known, or simply kept quiet? That's not what friends do, and, I believe, certainly not what is correct in business. Then again, looking at where our being true to ourselves got us in the end, maybe we were wrong.

These are tough questions to answer. By way of comparison, Steve Jobs was very unpopular for a time, and some might say unscrupulous in his dealings. But by staying true to his vision, he managed to stay in control and became an icon of what a great businessperson should aspire to emulate.

CHAPTER FIFTEEN

PRIDE & PREJUDICE

It may seem that the ride for the launch of the brand and our part in it as the UK contingent was serendipitous and lucky. Indeed, others attempted to dismiss our hard work setting up what was to become a well-oiled machine producing the premiere speciality sock brand by saying, 'Well you can't go wrong with such a great well-made product can you?" Perhaps the blood, sweat and tears are easily forgotten by those who didn't experience it first-hand. As minor shareholders our reward was only the one salary paid, not two, as I was debarred from being paid independently for any work. While it was on a needs must basis, and I shrugged my shoulders thinking it was only a principle, I think in the end this sowed the seed of the idea that what I contributed was therefore irrelevant. Sadly, I was forced to face up to the reality that not only was there still still a deep-down chauvinism in South Africa, but also that, by just scratching the surface of the opinions of many intolerant Republicans in the southern states of America, you easily revealed something similar; you are principally judged by your gender, colour, how much you are paid or how big your house is. Usually, the first question we were asked when we said we had bought a house in America was how much square footage it had, which we found bizarre as we genuinely didn't know or gave it a thought.

Living in Port Elizabeth in the backward and traditional Eastern Cape compared to the more liberal Cape Town and Western states, I had found women were reflections of their husbands' status. And while I am no prude, I was shocked at the levels of infidelity among notably white south Africans (though I suspect it was little different in the native population from my more limited first-hand experience). The divorce rate statistics in that country were horrific; about 9 out of 10 marriages ended in divorce. Although that did not excuse the terrible behaviour which I experienced from the women I met when I lived there, I could appreciate that given those sorts of statistics, if a woman could not hold onto her man, the consequences were not pretty.

They were not to know that, at my innermost core, as you may have gathered from my foreword, I value loyalty above almost anything else. I would not have dreamed of allowing any of their husbands to betray them or my own husband by having a casual fling. I viewed with contempt any husband who thought it simply fine to have affairs with other men's wives, or even if the other party was unmarried.

The tale of the "hand on the knee" of the boss of the South African Mohair factory reaching surreptitiously under the table to his secretary at the annual Christmas Party, which was recounted to me by her not in disgust, but with a sense of having achieved some kind of success, meant that I was sickened not only by the men's attitudes and behaviour but even worse by the way the women seemed to accept and even encourage it. She even went on to imply that she had attempted to have my loyal husband led astray by asking him to take a lone, unattached female employee of the sister mohair blanket factory to the event and if he would drive her home afterwards. She told me this on one of my rare visits back to see my husband, and even went so far as to tell me in a sort of confiding tone that although the lady was to have stayed at her house as an overnight guest, in the end she didn't want her to do so. It seemed a very unkind, bizarre thing for her to have suggested and furthermore it planted some horrible seed of doubt in my mind as the party occurred during the time, I had moved back to the UK leaving my husband alone.

I do not want to come across as "holier than thou", or someone that has never made any mistakes, I am human and I think that pride has indeed been my worst sin: both my pride in being British, and as a woman who has worked hard in business to get on using only my own graft and tenacity, not by having "slept with the boss" to get on. I did find the attitudes of others have often frustrated me and I am sure I often over-compensate before anyone could even think of treading me down.

This may have meant that I came across as an arrogant opinionated Brit, feeling I must fly the flag when abroad, defending every real or implied slight to my nationality and gender. I know that sometimes it has been truly horrible to step outside of my body and witness the unleashing of a self-destructive streak in me. I know I can have a cutting tongue when threatened, but it's easy to look back and reflect later that staying schtum and gracious might have been the wisest thing to do. I shoot from the hip and end up wounding both myself and, sadly, also those close to me, as they end up defending me to their cost.

I am saying this as a preamble to the final acts of my story. When we get to the final chapter you will see how this eventually came back to bite me in truly horrific circumstances.

As they say, 'hold that thought', as the worst is yet to come.

A note here also about alcohol and hypocrisy. One of the things that caused us irreverent, often irreligious Brits both surprise and amusement, was that we could not fail to notice a recurring theme wherever we went in America, especially throughout the southern states. This was the close juxtaposition of the town's liquor store and the place of worship. We joked that it made it so handy for the American churchgoer after listening to a pious sermon about the perils of the devilish brews, to pop next door to buy some supplies before going home to get properly wasted and shoot up the neighbourhood.

Having said that, as I write this, I do a feel a little vindicated by my comments, having just watched the truly horrific scenes of the Trump supporters incited to march on the capital and the subsequent interviews with some of them, which seemed to support my worst opinions about them.

To be fair, the bigotry and prejudice cut both ways. I lost count of the number of times when, after introduced as being British, the answer was nearly always, "Oh you drink warm beer over there don't you?" This was usually said in a derogatory manner. On one occasion I was told confidently and provocatively, "That's where you worship the Queen isn't it?"

It was exceedingly difficult when confronted with these slights, not to "bite back" with an acidic or defensive repost.

My aggressive reaction may also have had a lot to do with having been bullied and harassed through my childhood years for my posh accent and being an army officers' daughter forced to attend military schools among the children of the "other ranks" (and I say that without prejudice). It was unusual, to say the least, to have been sent to these local military schools on the various army bases, because, as officers' daughters, we more typically would have been packed off to exclusive private boarding schools like Roedean or Casterton back in England.

It is well known that children can be cruel, and my elder sister only recently told me that she was always having to look after me, trying to ensure that I did not get beaten up all the time in the playground. Being teased, kicked and humiliated over many years tends to bring out the worst in people, but also it has instilled a strong sense of justice. Should I ever see it happening to anyone else I get truly angry, and wade in with my protective mode fully engaged, no matter what the danger to myself personally, either physically or in terms of reputation. I just see red and cannot stand by and look on.

Even when my mother decided that we would return "up north" back in the UK, where her roots were, we were sent to a local school while living in Cumbria for a while. Once again, we experienced constant bullying in the first few weeks at the local school, at the hands of the pupils living in the rural farming area, all with rich "country accents". This led to all three sisters deciding to just not go to school for a whole winter term. Instead, we jaunted around the Lake District with our mother looking for a house to buy so we could relocate one last time when my father finally retired from military service and retrain as a probation officer in civvy street.

The truant office came round once, but to no avail, and eventually we settled in Lancashire, attending different local schools, but the bullying didn't stop there. After we ended up renting a dilapidated wing of a broken-down stately home, this, combined with our nice English accents led to us once again being pilloried for being snobs. The fact that it was freezing in winter as it cost a fortune to heat with the oil-fired boiler (ridiculously located in an outhouse from which the hot water pipe ran unlagged a few yards under the cobbled yard to the house) meant that we were extremely poor trying to keep up with the bills. Also, my fathers' job training as a probation officer was not well paid, so my mother did some district nursing which was also low paid to try and make ends meet. Humiliatingly, she even found additional work at a local public house, cleaning the toilets. This made the chants and abuse for being posh, and "stuck-up" at school even harder to take lying down. I remember one terrible day at the co-ed school I first attended when a group of girls decided it would be fun to drag me into a side cloakroom just off the main thoroughfare hallway and try to strip me of all my clothes, then push me naked (aged about 13 years at the time) into the limelight.

Panicked and fighting for my dignity as they clawed and ripped at my clothes, I remember biting one of the girls on the arm to try and escape the humiliation.

So, you can perhaps forgive me for not taking insults, or real or imagined slights very well in later life. I think I also get some of my feistiness from following in my fiercely protective mother's footsteps. While she was mainly powerless to protect us when at school, she did fight back in lioness mode if she was able to. She once confronted the 6-foot 4 father of a boy who had laid into us on the way home from school. When we arrived home crying and after showing her our bruises, and once she had ascertained where the boy lived, she immediately marched round with us in tow, and knocked on the door. When it was answered gruffly by the father, she refused to be intimidated and proceeded to verbally tear a strip off him regarding his son's behaviour. After some angry denial and initial protestations as he in turn automatically defended his child, he was shown the evidence as we cowered behind her. Looking at three little girls aged between 5 and 9 at, with tear-streaked faces, he could see that his bully son had indeed been at fault and agreed to "have words" with him. We almost felt sorry for him then as it was likely that he would be given more than a nice sit-down talk and dressing down from his rough, tough military father.

On another occasion, I remember my mother storming round to confront the primary school headmaster in the defence of a poor little girl who was punished and made a pariah of by him for such heinous misdeeds as not wearing the proper school uniform. In truth her family was so poor she looked as if she didn't even get enough to eat, let alone be properly clothed in the said uniform. For some unknown reason, the head had seemed to take some perverse pleasure in making her an example, so one day after we came home and told her that he had made the little girl stand up in the morning assembly and made a public example of her in front of the whole school, she snapped and marched off to confront him with a tirade. I think she wiped the floor with him, and, though he stopped bullying the little girl, it didn't go well for us, as he then made every attempt to get back at us and I was to bear the brunt of his petty vengeance sometime later.

Considering all the cruel treatment and hardships I have endured for being the person that I am, perhaps I can be forgiven for my continuing inability to keep my mouth shut or to "lie down quietly" in face of any threat or slight, despite the fact this has never gone well for me.

An example of this came later in my time in America, when my other half was away on trip to South Africa for the big charity presentation event.

We had been invited to our accountant's annual drinks party (another golfing buddy of the major US partner). The gathering was to celebrate yet another successful year and as a thank-you to his customers.

I was the sole remaining representative of our sock company, with the other partners all away at the big charity presentation event in South Africa. By this stage, the business was approaching the £6M mark in its fifth year of trading, so we were a significant customer of his. I felt it would be polite for at least one of us to attend. I was feeling rather lonely, and a bit left out. I dressed up and applied my make-up carefully as my armour. As the sole representative of both the company and the UK, I was quite nervous, and feeling at a bit of a low ebb from various things that had been happening, so I adopted a seemingly confident manner to try and compensate for the usual deep insecurities, which were never far below the surface,

Looking back, I must have had a foreboding that the polite smiles, and the supposedly friendly banter I typically encountered, was to manifest itself in the altogether more sinister and thinly veiled antagonism of some proud Americans towards their erstwhile adversary and enemy.

Without my husband to bolster my confidence and present a concerted British front, I arrived with a painted-on bright smile and forced myself to mingle and open some conversational gambits to the assembled guests, mostly husbands and wives. Armed with some Dutch courage after taking a few large swigs from a first glass of wine, I was introduced to a well-heeled pair and started chatting about a subject I knew a bit about, which also seemed "safe": my love and knowledge of wines. This came from personal experience of travelling on a wine-tasting tour of Stellenbosch in South Africa from our time over there, as well as sampling many different European and Antipodean (or "New World") wines over the years. The conversation started off innocently enough, as the couple opined that the wines of California were the best in the world. Then they swiftly moved onto the offensive but almost inevitable "warm beer" jibe. Stung by their condescension, I gave my standard response: "Well, you see, it's so you can actually taste how good it is." Then I went further: "And as the obvious wine buffs you seem to be, you will know that the best way to mask a truly dreadful wine is to chill it within an inch of its life – so the same is true of many American beers that have to be imbibed cold to make them palatable".

As you can imagine, this did not go down well, so, I gave what I hoped was a light-hearted, self-deprecating laugh and said, "But I am not a big beer expert, although I did sample some great brands in South Africa." I was also able to add that I had once installed some point-of-sale equipment in an outlet specialising in Belgian beers and had been able to sample and enjoy a few of these as well, though many were a little sweet for my taste, as they make many fruit-flavoured beers there.

It might have ended there, but I then made the mistake of professing a penchant for the odd whisky or two; I named my then favourite Glenkinchie and Bowmore. I was poised to recount a funny anecdote about the time when, staying in a Scottish hotel on one rainy afternoon, we had decided to work our way through all the whisky blends, served by a willing and complicit barman. As we ordered each new round ending with the customary "and one for yourself", he returned the favour by sneaking us double measures each time. But before I could get to that, I was abruptly cut dead by the husband loudly sneering – "I have tried ALL Scottish whiskies, and they are ALL shit!"

His wife looked at me with thinly veiled contempt as I struggled to regain my equilibrium. How could I possibly respond to this obviously rude, confrontational attempt to insult me. I must have turned a bright shade of red, and attempted a flustered exit from the situation, as I could see that this was a debate I was not going to come out of unscathed. I was alone and didn't want things turning nasty, so I swiftly excused myself to escape with the excuse of getting another glass of wine with a throwaway line: "Well I guess everyone has different tastes."

Feeling shaken and very uncomfortable, I didn't stay much longer; as soon as I was able, I thanked my host for the party and left to drive myself home (drink driving laws and limits were lax then). I cried all the way as, it was at that point I realised that, despite the success of the company we had built and having done our very best to settle in and embrace America as our home, I was horribly homesick and unhappy. I had little resilience left in me to pretend that the dismissive way that we, as the British partners, were treated, and I knew it was something I could not endure for much longer.

It had become increasingly obvious that, having got everything off to a flying start and successful venture, it was no longer necessary for them to woo or even be nice to us anymore. After the red carpet and initial hospitality shown to get us to come on board and bring the different nationalities together, we were now disposable commodities. Sadly, I only saw it at this stage, and my husband either did not see it, or couldn't because he had always wanted to settle in the USA. Being so invested in the company we had built; he didn't want to acknowledge that the not-so-subtle sea change in attitude towards us had begun.

Once back in the safety and sanctuary of our own home, I started to bitterly reflect on the past and recalled ironically that several years earlier, before we came to America, when staying at the house of our south African friends and would-be partners, I had persuaded them to put aside their misgivings and agree to come on board as they were being hesitant. They were voicing their main objection, that the US partner was not to be trusted. To my regret, considering how things eventually turned out, I remember defending the partner saying yes, he was a businessman and would act in his own interests, but that they should not let this stand in the way of joining the partnership because we would ensure that the company was structured in such a way that no one partner would have overall control.

After that conversation, my husband astutely made sure that when the company was formed with the various shareholders, the two major shareholding contingents, the US partner and the South Africans, would have equal and hence non-controlling percentages each and the main bulk of the shares. This was supposed to be a safeguard, meaning that neither one could overrule the other and that at least one of the other minor shareholders, would also need to agree if one major shareholder wanted a collaboration on a vote.

It seemed to be a watertight plan, but we never would have countenanced the possibility that the major partners, Tinker (US) & Tailor (SA), (and allegedly our friends) might band together and, with the help of one of the minor ones (I shall just call him Brutus), would secretly plot and gang up on us in later years.

CHAPTER SIXTEEN

THE THIN END OF THE WEDGE

Under pressure from the other partners, we rolled over in the end, and had agreed to hire sales reps on a commission basis. I'll admit that a number of them had been instrumental in expanding the business and not just riding on the back of what we had already trail blazed. We reasoned that they could be helpful in being the feet on the ground going into these retail establishments, and instrumental in adding value, for instance by training the sales staff on the unique features of the brand and introducing new styles.

After a while we decided to invite all the reps to a sales conference in order to congratulate them, inspire them to greater endeavours, talk about new initiatives and get to know them better in person.

We were to have hosted the welcoming party at our house on the lake, where we had started building an entertainment area in our basement leading out onto a garden area. We had also installed a separate bedroom, bathroom, and kitchenette downstairs so we could have visitors, partners or our friends and family come and visit us. We wanted them to be able to be comfortable and to enjoy their own space when staying with us if they wanted. They would be able to get up, make a coffee or tea in the night or early morning if jet-lagged, and take a shower without having to creep about waiting for other people to arise.

It was a huge undertaking, as when we purchased the house, it had a large unfinished area in the basement with a rough concrete floor. So, we started by having a builder make partitions for the guest bedroom, kitchenette and bathroom which needed plumbing to be installed. This involved unanticipated obstacles, as many of you who have ever undertaken any building works will ruefully acknowledge.

This was to be the case for us also, as we found out that the house was built on top of a layer of thick granite, which meant that there were many days of hideously loud and protracted drilling to be able to sink the additional recesses required into the hard bedrock foundations. The builder went through a series of expensive drill bits. Inevitably, this also incurred additional costs and delays in the completion date we wanted, which was to be finished in time to host the planned sales conference.

We did manage to get the bedroom and bathroom and most of the kitchenette finished, as we expected the South African friends and partners to stay with us and we wanted to return the hospitality that they had extended to us when we stayed with them in Cape Town. I rushed about madly, buying home comforts like an additional coffee maker, coffee cups, an assortment of cutlery and an expensive new bed with tasteful bedding and soft matching towels, to make their anticipated stay with us as comfortable as I could. It was also necessary, as our main guest bedroom and bathroom in the main part of the house was typically occupied by one of the other small shareholders (later to become Brutus); during the week, as I've mentioned. He usually drove up on a Monday morning and stayed with us overnight until Friday when he drove back home.

However, the delays meant the main entertainment space was not going to be ready to accommodate the reps party and conference, so we were reluctantly forced to ask if the US partner could host it at his spacious house and grounds. It did mean that his wife had to scramble a bit to empty a garage space that would house the drinks and tables for speeches, but they were able to get her scout group to help clear it out and get it ready. We felt bad about it; personally, I felt on the back foot and thought we had somehow "failed", and I hated having to ask someone else to host it, especially at that time when I felt that our relationship had started to become a little rocky. Maybe if I had been more confident that the reps would have understood that things were a bit less than perfect, we should have just bitten the bullet, but I was extremely nervous that it would not be good enough, so I persuaded my husband to cry off us hosting it.

When the event started, it got off to a bit of a bad start from our perspective, as there was an issue with the sales assistant we had personally hired. It appeared that the drinks for the party, which we had asked her to handle, would not arrive in time (when in fact she had it all under control). However, as she was our choice of staff member, it seemed to become another opportunity to get at us and find fault.

I knew she would not let us down, but as there was a bit of a breakdown in communication at the eleventh hour, it was extremely stressful and ended up being quite unpleasant for us to have to try and defend her until the supplies arrived.

But the hurtful part of the conference occurred just days before the arrival of the South Africans, as I was enthusiastically explaining all my preparations for them were in place so they could stay in our newly appointed guest suite. I had brought forward its completion by dipping into our dwindling bank account to purchase the expensive new bed, along with the carefully picked out bedding and towels to match and some thoughtful toiletries in case anything had been forgotten. However, they preferred to accept the US partner's counteroffer of hospitality. We felt very slighted and disappointed by their choice. Just looking back on it, I am in tears once again remembering this rejection of our hospitality. It did seem to be very strange, and a deliberate insult made to distance themselves from us in favour of the other shareholder.

It may have been that they simply wanted to spare me the stress, as indeed they had previously witnessed at first-hand an occasion when I hosted a meal for all the partners, which was not an outstanding success. Once again, my stupid pride had come into play, as I stupidly insisted on doing a full day's work before rushing home at 5pm to prepare a meal for 10 people.

I had at least had the foresight to make some Tiramisu for dessert the night before. I had practised this before, using a Jamie Oliver recipe and it had turned out well. Unfortunately, on this occasion, as I had put it in the fridge overnight, it was rather solid when it was served, and, to my shame didn't have that melty coffee creaminess expected.

As you may gather from my Sluts' Suppers anecdotes, I am not, and have never purported to being an accomplished chef. Consequently, I panic and over-cater whenever I am doing the cooking, but I really was trying in my silly proud way to show that I could be the "hostess with the mostest".

In the end the entire meal wasn't that great, but neither was it terrible. However, I remember the US shareholders wife, refusing to eat my "safe" prawn cocktail starter, as she said she wasn't very hungry.

It was therefore doubly humiliating that my dessert, for which I had high hopes to redeem any shortcomings in the previous courses, being too cold when served directly from the fridge; and so sadly, no-one enjoyed. It was only when, clearing up the significant leftovers after everyone had left, I tasted it at room temperature and it had finally attained the creamy loveliness expected (but too late to save my shame). I was so upset, as we had indeed had some delicious meals at others' houses and I felt I had let myself, my husband, and Britain down, all at the same time.

I have had other meal disasters, (many years before Bridget Jones's iconic 'blue string' soup), when I made a fruit cocktail as a party dessert. Kiwi fruit were a bit of a novelty way back in the 80's, and I didn't know that you had to peel them. So, I had just chopped them up, hairy jackets and all, and tossed them into the bowl along with the rest of the assorted fruits I had bought. Then, as I didn't have any real idea of how you made a fruit salad, I decided to throw in a few miniature liqueurs I had found lurking in the back of a cupboard. I think I had been confusing this with the ingredients of a sherry trifle. Also, then, as now, I felt everything is improved by the addition of a little (or a lot) of booze. Subsequently, with the addition of an eclectic combo of Blue Curacao and Bols Banana liqueur, when the lights were turned down low in party style, it had the unusual and slightly alarming effect of emitting a weird sci-fi fluorescent turquoise glow.

However, thus is a measure of true friends, as my glowing, hairy fruit salad was eaten without complaint, just a bit of laughter and teasing, so it just remains another amusing memory. It is right up there in my list of entertaining disasters with my Brandy Alexander; at the end of an evening, having run out of wine, I ended up bizarrely whizzing up cream and brandy using a hand rotary whisk, with both my head and mixing bowl placed under the living room carpet. The idea was to prevent the mixture flying off everywhere, but of course it must have been a comical sight to behold, especially as I emerged with my face and hair splattered with big blobs of the mixture.

I once had a fondue party (hasn't everyone?), but as usual it ended up being a bit of an improvisation. I had a fondue set (a Christmas gift from a relative as they were ubiquitous at that time). I also had cheese, wine and some bread for my impromptu dinner gathering, but didn't have the necessary methylated spirit to fuel the burner device. Nor did I know where to get some, other than by mugging some unsuspecting tramp on a park bench. Undeterred by small details like this, I found a bottle of vodka and thought, well, its alcohol, isn't it? Having found a solution to the problem, I filled up the little container dish and set it alight with a lighted match and a big fanfare, despite the sense of danger and occasion that was somewhat akin to setting off a firework when lighting the blue touch paper and standing well back. As it happens, it was perfectly fine, and another great evening was had by all, one which my friends still talk about fondly, despite a little of teasing aimed in my direction. I know it is done with love, and I do not feel diminished by it, which I am sorry to say was not the case with the awful shareholders dinner party.

Only one of the minor shareholders, along with his lovely wife, who were both great cooks, set an example of the difference between true and false friendship; they ate the meal and even proffered some compliments. (Even though I knew they were not deserved, they were made kindly and much appreciated).

I recall their support on a previous occasion, when we had all taken a trip to evaluate and discuss adding a sportswear line of garments to the brand and I had made a spicy prawn dish for everyone. I felt sure I had taken out all the fiery seeds from the chilis, before chopping them into small pieces and adding to the mix, but it was truly so hot as to be virtually inedible. Again, this couple proved their friendship, valiantly not only eating their initial portion, but even coming back for a second helping. I think they did it to make me feel better, and for that I was profoundly grateful, even though I am sure it burnt their mouths.

Of all the partners and friends, we knew from that time, they remain the only ones that we keep in touch with. I do miss them and the great meals we shared at their house.

True loyalty and friendship cannot be bought, and there is nothing I will not do for my friends in return.

The sales conference was a success in the end, but it was at this point that it was not just me that noticed the change in the attitude of our partners, but others also noticed that something was not quite right with the happy brand of brothers.

This became clear when, as I was saying my piece on the closing evening, thanking the reps and raising a toast to everyone's hard work, I was humiliated by being interrupted and cut dead in full flow while mid-sentence, by the South African partner as I was attempting to publicly acknowledge the contribution of the reps. It was even more hurtful and galling especially as I was genuinely trying to admit in some way that I was wrong about appointing the reps, (of course they were not to know that I had initially blocked it), but I also wanted to show that I and my husband were key contributors and partners in the success of the brand. But we were to be denied that as well, and as I was forced to sit down mortified that everyone could see I that had been dismissed as not worthy. I could also see that he wanted to deny me taking any credit by rudely cutting short my little speech.

Later, one of the reps, privately and unbidden, said that he had been appalled and saddened by the way we were treated, thus proving that my increasing concerns were not simply paranoia, but a sign of what was to come.

CHAPTER SEVENTEEN

THE END OF A DREAM

The business was still doing well, and we had worked hard to try and make our permanent home in America. We had made a few friends, generally through business contacts, but there was not much time when building the business for attending any social events or taking up any hobbies that might lead to some new input into our lives. In the limited free time we had, which was only at weekends (typically we didn't ship orders then), we devoted our time to working on the additions to the house. We were proud of our large house on the lake as, back in the UK, only the well-to-do could afford such a house and we had certainly never had anything so grand before. The music/playroom was nearing completion, and the special guest suite had been made habitable in readiness for the aborted visit from the South African partners, so we continued to cling to our American dream, hoping that we would have a happy and successful permanent home there.

In the five years since our optimistic arrival, which could be likened to pilgrims alighting from the Mayflower, we had thrown everything into making this second attempt at starting a new life in another country a success. We had used all the equity we had brought with us from the sale of the home in the UK, as we had needed to put down a significant deposit on the house on the lake. After initially renting a property, my husband wanted to ensure that this immigration (unlike the first attempt) would stick. I believe he thought that, once we had purchased a beautiful home, we would be permanently wedded to that country. I still had some misgivings about taking such a step, but felt I had to try because of my guilt that I had somehow unwittingly sabotaged our previous attempt by not being able to make my business a success in South Africa.

I attempted to put off the decision to purchase the house by asking the estate agent to make a significantly lower offer to the owner, but as houses on the lakeside were in very short supply, and because our first offer had been almost immediately accepted, in the end we secured the deal. Once again, we started almost from scratch having left nearly everything behind in the UK except for a few nice pieces of furniture we had acquired in South Africa. In the end we must have spent hundreds of hours and thousands of dollars on the house itself, plus perhaps $1,000 more spent on buying plants for the enormous but largely uncultivated back garden (or yard as the Americans call it) which led down to the lake. My hobby, whenever I had a spare moment, was gardening. It was a joy to have the opportunity to transform this rocky landscape into the beautiful English garden of my dreams. Previously I had had little or no garden in our tiny UK properties, but still always managed to get outside, planting some tiny shrubs, some roses and some colourful bedding plants and even a small tree or two as I have always loved them and had once trained as a volunteer tree warden many years before. Whenever I was unhappy or stressed at work, I would buy a few "planties" as my husband called them, and, after the ensuing digging, trowelling and generally throwing rocks about, managed to get them in just the right place to be admired from our house; it always relaxed me and helped put things into perspective. I consequently spent nearly every weekend toiling over our extensive but extremely steep and rocky garden.

It was such hard work and so absorbing, that it temporarily allowed my feverish and occasionally paranoid thoughts to dissipate. It also allowed me to fall into bed at the end of the day, tired, but happy. It was in only this area of my life that I felt I had complete control. I took pleasure in having achieved something worthwhile that was all mine and that no-one could criticise me for or tell me what to do with. This was typically British, I suppose; it is so often said that an Englishman's home is his castle.

It was not the most fun though, as in the oppressively hot and humid summers there, it was usually boiling hot outside, and, with the southern states' tendency to have that sort of nasty high humidity, it was very unpleasant hacking away at the hard granite ground in order to make the footholds in which to plant my English rose garden and the few carefully chosen trees which I had struggled to source in North Carolina. I had always loved Laburnum in the UK, and I had planted one at every home we moved to and eagerly awaited the arrival in late spring of the gorgeous cascades of golden sunshiny, yellow racemes. It always made me smile and lifted my spirits just gazing on its beauty.

In addition to the sourcing difficulties (as Laburnum was not really suited to the climate and thin granite soil), whenever I had anything new to plant, this required frequent exhausting trips back up a 45-degree incline in the high heat and humidity which persisted for much of the summer months. I always did this in order to find just the right place for the perfect layout and optimum viewing aspect from our deck or lounge window, for each tree, bush, plant, water feature or statue.

The air-conditioning in the house was subsequently very welcome, as after every trek back up the slope in order to check the positioning of each new addition to my garden, I needed a cooling off period and frequent cold drinks. Being unused to the climate, without these rest intervals, I would surely have suffered heat stroke. This did however mean that even planting just one new bush or locating each landscape feature took about five times as long as it would have done in the temperate and much smaller garden areas back home. Once I had cooled off sufficiently to attempt yet another exodus into the heat, this involved slipping and sliding back down the roughly hewn steps or sheer slippery slope so the item could be moved (usually just a few inches to an altered position), then once again, going back up the hill to make a final check. Then once again back down the hillside carrying a specially designed implement called a mattock (basically, a pickaxe to you and me) to dig the hole required. The topsoil was usually just a rough dusting of material with hard granite underneath. I had already broken a few spades and forks in the losing battle between implement and the unforgiving land.

This sweaty ordeal was made worse by the abundance of mosquitos that prolifically bred in the lake. They were ferocious in pursuit of their tasty meal of sweet British blood. I therefore had to be covered from head to toe in impenetrable clothing. Even a special long-sleeved T-Shirt sent to me by my dear mother, which was supposed to be mozzie-proof, was bitten through by the little blighters. It was especially galling as our neighbours and American friends who lived on the other side of the lake said that they never got bitten at all! I concluded that, after having been inoculated by years of this happening, their bodies no longer set off the alarm bell; the histamine response of the swelling and intense itching I suffered whenever I was dined upon by the anopheles ladies. (It is only the females that bite: they need a meal of blood to produce their eggs). From my father's work in Singapore, I did know a lot about these little pests, but I was still driven almost crazy by the buzzing clouds that seemed to appear as if by magic whenever I appeared in the garden. It was to have been expected in retrospect, due to our insistence on buying a property so close to the lake, but we totally underestimated the extent to which we would be plagued. Undeterred, I continued in dogged, single-minded (some might say bloody minded) pursuit of my goal.

My husband had been a keen water-skier in the UK and South Africa, so we had also duly applied for planning permission to have a dock built to allow us to keep a boat for that purpose, or just for some merry jaunts on what were called "floating gin palaces". Looking out on the lake also fulfilled a dream for me; wherever we ended up living, I always wanted to have "a room with a view", if possible, including some sort of water. So, I had been thrilled about managing to secure a house with lake views.

However, we now arrive at the point when the small slow, tortuous pinpricks and increasingly uncomfortable tensions in the work environment started to increasingly prey on my mind. I started to feel unappreciated, as the antagonism seemed to be mainly aimed in my direction, I felt that I was persona non grata and no-one likes to feel like that. My escape mechanism was immersing myself in improving our home, swapping a hot tub for installation of a new glass door so I could look out over the garden, (which to my relatives back home was madness as having one seemed the pinnacle of bourgeois middle class dreams of success). However, the pleasure I took in making a lovely home and garden became less and less of an escape from those insidious creeping feelings of being unwelcome and criticised at work.

I remember, as the atmosphere worsened, driving to a garden centre to purchase a load of cheerful bedding plants when I was feeling particularly low after a bad week at the business. I thought they would have the usual effect of lifting my spirits. However, as a sign of how things were really getting to me, I ended up in a desperate fit of hysterical crying after my wheelbarrow, filled with my booty of carefully selected plants, tipped over on the precarious descent down the slope, shedding all the contents as they tumbled downhill, squashing stems and petals as they bounced. In normal circumstances, I would have been a tad upset, but would have just picked them up consoling myself that they would be in essence unharmed when planted and watered into position. Instead, I just sank down onto the path, burst into tears and was unable to stop. When he discovered me in this sorry state, my husband was a bit frustrated and mystified as to why I was so distraught, but he did pragmatically retrieve the fallen plants, put them back in the wheelbarrow and take it down the rest of the slope to the prepared flower bed waiting below. But the usually restorative effect of planting them failed to lift my spirits, and I remained in a dejected mood, as if under a dark cloud for the rest of the weekend.

It was bad enough myself feeling this way, but it was exacerbated over time when their animosity seemed to spill over in my husband's direction. I guess we were a "package", and he to an extent had to defend me (even though he did not always do so if he did not agree with my position).

I think the tensions started to eat away at him as well; it culminated with him also falling out of favour when there was a nasty incident between him and the US partner. It happened after he had accused the warehouse manager (who was employed at the main yarn company) of incompetence after an expensive large flat screen television only recently purchased, had been stolen from our offices. It was intended to be used to play the videos of the presentations at our charity in South Africa to any visiting reps or to customers and stakeholders. It was the warehouse manager's job to go round the perimeter at the end of each day and secure all the side doors adjoining both warehouses. It had previously been brought to his attention that sometimes this had not been done and that the door had been found unlocked the next day. As there was no sign of a break in, the blame and responsibility were not unreasonably (or so we thought), placed at his door.

A distressing scene ensued as after the US partner came across after learning of the theft and hearing of my husband's allocation of where the blame lay; there were some heated exchanges, after which I heard a loud crash coming from my husband's office. Rushing over, fearing some terrible accident, I saw that he had in frustration, thrown a cup he had been drinking out of across the room; it now lay shattered in tiny pieces against the opposite wall. This was unlike him, being normally a very calm rational person, but I think again it was a sign that the undercurrents of conflict and the attempts to wrest control away from us were getting to him too.

While I am certain he did not throw it at the shareholder, it was an upsetting and unfortunate event which, to my mind, marked a final turning point against us. And, sure enough, not long after that, a plot to oust us was discovered, unfortunately by me.

My suspicions had been aroused not only by the increasingly poisonous atmosphere whenever I was around the US partner, but that now seemed to have started to pervade through to his staff. I was telephoned one day by his right-hand salesperson (and a friend of ours who we had enjoyed time in Paris with and had stayed at each other's houses and had joined her and her partner at a beach house one summer weekend). She worked in the adjacent building at the yarn company and had called me to ask if we had a printer she could borrow, as hers was malfunctioning and she needed to print off some urgent documents. Always anxious to help anyone, and as we had in turn been helped with the use of the other business's equipment in the beginning, I decided to go across personally and see what the issue was. Coming from an IT background, I was good at identifying and remedying any computer problems but took along a zip drive so, if I failed, I could copy off and then print the documents for her myself when back in my own office. As I cheerily breezed into her office, which had an adjoining door to the main US shareholder's, I started asking how she was and told her I was here to check out the printer problem, and about my plan B if that didn't work. I had known her a while and she had worked closely with my husband, so I was rather mystified when she seemed uncomfortable that I had shown up. She answered in monosyllables to my questions and kept glancing over to the open door between the offices. I figured that her boss must have been in there, so I thought maybe it was because she didn't want to admit she had a problem, or that I was interrupting her work, but that seemed silly, as I was only trying to help. However, eventually as I became increasingly confused; feeling that I was not welcome, I beat a hasty retreat saying she could call me if she was still stuck for anything.

I once again realised that things were not as they should be. In previous times, I might have expected her boss, the US shareholder, to have popped his head round the door to say hi, and I would normally have done the same if it were not for the peculiar behaviour I had just witnessed from yet another supposed friend of ours.

A bit shaken by this, I mentioned the perplexing incident to my husband, but he seemed to dismiss it as just my paranoia, saying that she had probably just been busy and that I should not have just shown up like that.

Once again, it seemed I was the wrong person, in the wrong place, at the wrong time. I felt incredibly sad and quite alone.

But things did not improve, and the next week I had come into work a bit earlier, as I had not slept well and had a lot to do.

CHAPTER EIGHTEEN

BRUTUS

As it was a Monday, we expected the minor shareholder, the runner, to arrive at our offices as usual around 10.30 am as he had a long commute in. On my own arrival into the office I wanted to make a speedy start on my task list, but I discovered that we had run out of packing tape. As I needed to prepare some special sample orders up, I thought I would pop to the other company warehouse through the adjoining door that separated the two businesses, so I could borrow a few rolls to tide us over to be replaced when our delivery arrived.

I got my tape and had a short cheery chat with the young warehouse guy I had always got on well with. As an African American employed in the Deep South, I always felt he was looked down on a little by the others and, as was my wont, I always went out of my way to be pleasant and acknowledge him whenever our paths crossed. As I was about to depart back to our warehouse, I happened to glance through his warehouse door which opened out onto the rear carpark of the yarn company. Imagine my surprise, as it was only 8.30 or 9 am at the latest, when I spotted the car of the runner shareholder parked up there, not only not in our own front carpark, nor the front carpark of the yarn company, but out of sight round the back in the area designed for deliveries.

How odd, I thought, why has he come in so early and parked there instead of in front of our offices as usual? Was there some shareholders' meeting I was unaware of taking place, and why, if that was indeed the case, had at least my husband not been invited to it? He hadn't mentioned anything to me, but I thought maybe it had slipped his mind or he just hadn't thought to mention it. I never expected to be invited to any of these in any case.

However, I thought it odd and, as my husband was in his office, it was obvious that he had not been invited to any meeting that morning. As COO, one might have expected that he would have been, or at least to be aware of any such meetings going on.

I made my way back to our side of the warehouse, and went into my husband's office, to tell him what I had seen and to ask if he knew of any reason why some private meeting might be taking place that day.

He looked a bit bemused by this information and said he had no knowledge of any meeting having been arranged. To be sure, it is perfectly feasible that one shareholder might have something to say privately to another, but the secretive car parking and early doors meeting seemed odd.

Already my female intuition was telling me that this was not some innocent meeting, so, when he made an appearance later driving his car round to our offices as if he had just arrived, I asked in as casual way I could muster, "Did you have a meeting with X this morning?" To this he looked a bit taken aback as to how I might have known this and muttered something about him having had something he wanted to run past him. I left it at that but had a nagging sense of doom. I was determined to get to the bottom of anything that might have been going on. It seemed underhand and unnecessary, as I have always been totally transparent with everyone and expected everyone to act in the same way.

It was then I decided that, as I had access to all the IT system passwords, I would try and see if I could find out anything that might have been going on by opening all the company emails over the recent few weeks. While I would not normally use my access to look at anyone else's emails, something just did not feel at all right. Allied to this we had heard, at relatively short notice, about an upcoming visit planned by the South African shareholders in a week or so, to hold a rather unexpected and extraneous board meeting. I wanted to have a heads up on anything that might be going on that we needed to know about before they arrived, as I just could not shake off a horrible feeling that it was not going to be something that would be good for us.

Trust me, I am not proud of the covert actions that I took on that fateful day. I felt terrible and a little ashamed to do something like this, as being underhand is not in my nature, but I desperately hoped that I would just be reassured that, if any correspondence had occurred, it would be simply the usual round of intercompany emails, and just business as usual. This would then allow me to put aside my worries that the upcoming board meeting was something to be concerned about.

Having made the decision to investigate and put my mind at rest, I gained access to all the outgoing emails and replies and was dismayed and shocked when I quickly came across one between all the friends of Carlotta; in fact, it involved Carlotta himself, who I previously referred to as Tinker, but with Tailor and the original chain originating from the one I refer to as Brutus.

Notably neither my husband, nor our friend, the other smaller shareholder, were cc-ed, which alerted me to think that perhaps there might be something odd going on. So, it was on that fateful and life-changing day, that I, in great fear and trepidation, guiltily opened the email.

The phrase "My blood ran cold" was literally true as I read the email written by Brutus to the other parties. The subject of the email was us, which was a terrible realisation, and I almost fainted in shock when I read it and the reply from the other partners.

The key part of the first email hit me like an axe to my head:

"{My name} has to go, and {My husband's name} has to also."

I read, and re-read the line in disbelief, not actually believing it said what I thought it had. Surely no, it could not possibly be saying that Brutus was asking for us to be dismissed from running the company we had worked so hard at building, and for us to be discarded at this successful high point like some used pieces of toilet paper. And this, coming from someone who had stayed at our house as a friend and partner?

With my mind reeling in shock., I tried desperately to somehow minimise the implications and severity of what he was proposing. I thought maybe they thought that it was just me that was superfluous to requirements, and that perhaps in some people's mind, maybe that was OK. I knew I had caused some friction in my refusal to roll over to some of their suggestions. But my husband also? What had he done to deserve this? As COO he had been doing such a brilliant job of running the company. Surely, they could not be considering dispensing with his services as well.

Then my thoughts switched from my own hurt feelings and disappointment to what his reaction would be when he heard this. God no! How awful a burden I felt considering that sharing this treachery with him, it would kill him, or at least severely wound his pride and faith in human nature, and worse, in his friends and partners.

I was so conflicted. I knew he would be angry with me for having abused my powers by reading the email in the first place, and frankly at that terrible moment, I dearly wished I had not.

What could I do? What should I do? What would you have done in the circumstances?

Having never fainted in all my life, I truly thought at that point that I might pass out with the shock. I think the way I felt could only be compared to a wife finding out about her husbands' infidelity, or a husband arriving home early, only to find his wife in bed with another man, like poor Smiley in the Le Carré novel.

What would we do? Where would we go? What options did we have? What would happen to our beloved cats, who had already endured one round of six months' quarantine when we brought them back to the UK from South Africa. One of them had also nearly died on the longer flight and ordeal involved in getting to the USA, as they had been shipped crated, and left negligently without water on the long journey. All these terrible thoughts went through my head like my life flashing before me while dying a humiliating, shameful death.

I forced myself to read the reply from the other shareholders as I thought, surely, they would be as horrified as me, and would reprimand him sharply for suggesting such a thing. I dearly hoped that things were not as bad as I had thought, and that their reply would profess loyalty to us and would countermand my terrible conclusion that there was a massive plot to oust us from the business and sound the death knell on our lives in America.

Taking a deep breath to try to steady myself, even though my chest felt so tight I could not seem to get any air into my lungs, and willing it not to be happening, I steeled myself to read the reply, still hoping against hope that it would all turn out to be some terrible misunderstanding.

But again, the depth of the betrayal was finally revealed in all its sickening reality. It went something like this:

Tailor replied, "'Well that's as maybe, but we still have a business to run.'"

Hardly a strong rebuttal, was it? It could have been worse, but in truth, not much. It proved that we were indeed no longer welcome, only that some way had to be engineered to dispense with us but designed so that it would not damage the business.

The die was cast; it was all over but the shouting. It all became horribly clear in an instant that this was the reason for the extraneous meeting that was, if not to sign our immediate death warrant, but to start the tortuous walk of shame during which it would be made clear our services were now superfluous to requirements and could be done away with at a stroke, now we had done all the hard work and the business success was secured.

Those of you if you based in the UK will no doubt be reading this and thinking, surely that cannot legally be allowed to happen. But sadly, certainly in the USA, when it comes to shareholders attaining a majority vote, anyone can be dispensed with, and without severance or indeed any notice or any form of compensation, leaving them only the ability to take with them their shares when they leave.

I had endured many setbacks and disappointments in my life up to that time, in both my business and personal life, but this was truly the worst day of my life. Could any day after that be more destructive to the spirit than that?

But kind readers, there were worse days that we had to endure to come in the following few months.

It now gets extremely hard for me to continue with my story, as the hurt and angst all comes back like a re-opened wound. As I relive the events that follow, I will be typing on through a mist of tears, just so I can finish the tale of those final horrific days that were the end of our dream.

Being in possession of this indisputable evidence and immersed irrevocably in thoughts of the true horror of what was to transpire, I battled with myself on what to do next, in an agony of indecision.

I dreaded having to tell my husband what I had just read, but how could I not? Would I just wait for the day of the board meeting and let him walk into a nightmare, where after some character assassination of his wife, he would be told that I was to be debarred from the company's business with immediate effect, or would he also be told to prepare to depart?

Eventually I managed to get unsteadily to my feet. White as a sheet, I tottered slowly down the corridor each step taking me closer to the horror of what I was about to wreak on my unsuspecting husband. I felt as if I was being taken to the gallows.

Once I had entered his office through the usually open doorway, I turned and slowly closed the door behind me. I stood there leaning on the door in case I fell and waited for him to look up, not trusting myself to speak lest I break down. I think I was still hoping that the cup of poison could be taken from me. He was my rock and always seemed to be able to fix anything and reassure me that, whatever happened, everything would be fine no matter what silliness I had got myself into. I hated myself for being about to destroy his life. I was still desperately clinging to a glimmer of hope that there would be a simple explanation or a way out of this with honour and dignity for us.

The terrible moment came when, hearing the door close and finishing what he was doing on his PC, he looked up and saw my haunted countenance.

He saw that I had a terribly similar look to the time when, on another incredibly sad day, I had shouted out "Oh NO!!" NO!!" in dismay and utter sadness when I heard the news that my dear friend had unexpectedly passed away from her malignant brain tumour. Rushing into my office on that day, he saw the same look of despair and utter sadness painted across my face.

I was leant against the door jamb as if it were the only thing keeping me upright. Getting to his feet and quickly coming across, as he asked – "What's wrong?" He must have assumed from the way I looked that someone else was dead, or that I had been diagnosed with some terrible incurable illness.

I could hardly bring myself to speak, but after a pause which seemed like an eternity, I said with a trembling voice "I think you need to take a look at something".

I showed him the email and the reply, and his reaction as I feared, was indeed horrible to behold. Like me, he kept reading and re-reading the words with a look of total incomprehension on his face, and, as I had done, rapidly went through the stages of grief: denial, anger, bargaining, depression, and acceptance.

He quickly moved on from the denial stage as he struggled to reformulate the words to make them not read the way they did, to find some way to slant the tone or content to come up with a benign message, but then his hurt turned to anger, which was briefly directed at me. He sharply asked. "How did you come by this?" I felt terrible about my methods but feeling defensive as the messenger and harbinger of doom, I was in fearful dread wanting to somehow not to have anything make how I felt any worse.

So, I did something that I never do, and that is to lie, so I said that I had stumbled across it when doing some routine email maintenance. To this day, I am not sure what was in fact the truth, as my actions before finding the email, have faded in my memory in comparison to the horror of what was to follow.

I hope I will get some sympathy from you; I had thought immediately after discovering the dreadful words that I had had no business looking in the first place. Worse than that, I had brought doom and destruction upon us by so doing, but it was done, and could not be undone. I could not unread the words I had seen or pretend that I could just carry on as normal, waiting in dread until the spectre of the guillotine loomed even larger on the arrival of the partners for the meeting that I felt for sure had been called to dismiss either me alone or us both.

I have thought so many times about that dreadful day and my decision to take matters into my own hands, thinking that, if I had let events take their course, things might have taken a different tack. But now I will never know. Maybe if I had not opened Pandora's Box, minds may have been changed, or some less destructive way may have been planned for our fate by the others, but all that remains as an irrevocable fact is that it did destroy our lives from that day on.

More than 12 years hence, there are still the ripples of the tsunami that I set in motion on that fateful day, as we still have not recovered from the consequences of the wheels set in motion either financially (as we ended up losing everything), or emotionally. I still often wake up from a terrible nightmare filled with memories of rejection and have remained forever scarred by the remorse, feelings of regret and low self-esteem that have dogged my later attempts to rebuild a new life and career.

With his head in his hands, my husband just looked destroyed. Worse than that, alongside the feelings of despair and the horror of the betrayal, we were now armed with the horrible knowledge of what was likely to come, but we were honestly at a loss about what to do now the cat was out of the bag. To confront our partners with what we had learned would mean that I would be discovered in my wrongdoing, and what would that serve to achieve? Would the ensuing row only hasten the end, so that it would come in an even more uncontrolled way? Should we just pretend that nothing was amiss and dumbly be led to our slaughter like lambs?

I desperately wanted some guidance, and some reassurance that, even when faced with what surely was irrefutable proof of the dark forces gathering against us, there might be some way to redemption. If there was indeed no hope of some light or rescue, I wanted that final nail to be driven into our hearts before we could come to any decision on what we could or should do. So, despite my husband's protestations, I said we should ask the remaining minor shareholder (who seemed to be our last remaining friend and advocate), to look at the email and its reply and tell us in a more objective way that what we feared it said was indeed the confirmation of my biggest fears.

I felt 100% sure that he would be totally in the dark as to the plans of the friends of Carlotta and did feel guilty about dragging him into the morass, but in the end, as I argued to my husband, it would be inevitable that he would eventually find out, so he might as well confirm our conclusions and be given a heads-up now. I did not want to ask him to pick a side, but to remain neutral and in apparent ignorance for his sake. I was cognisant of the fact that bringing him into it, when he had a family to feed and mortgage to pay was perhaps selfish of us. He was also an integral part of a sister business selling specialised medical socks, so his livelihood could possibly be endangered by us putting him in the difficult position of having a conflict of loyalties.

We decided that we would not ask him to do that, but that we should ask him simply to give his honest opinion, and perhaps suggest what he thought we should do if he were in our place.

After we had called him in, he in turn looked a little worried by our serious tone and deathly pallor. We just wordlessly asked him to read the email and then the reply so he could be unbiased as to the interpretation that he put on it.

Watching his face, I saw the same expressions I had seen before on my husband's. It transformed from curiousness to disbelief and a sort of denial. Then he even looked at me, almost as if somehow, I had made the email up myself.

He looked back and forth, and when he seemed not to believe what was before him, I asked if he had any inkling of what was behind it. I was not accusatory, as he was a firm friend who we saw often. We also knew that, even as a minor non-executive partner of the business, he was not really a part of the 'friends of Carlotta', inner circle. He was invited to main board meetings and, from time to time, the launch and development of the brand allowed to give his opinion on various aspects of the business with his great depth of experience and knowledge. But he also felt, as he once confided in us, that he was not treated with the respect he thought he deserved, and that often his suggestions were dismissed out of hand, but later, annoyingly, taken up when suggested by one of inner circle.

I did not suspect him of anything malign, but I wondered if he had heard anything negative about us from the other partners, or if in any way he might have seen something amiss. But his shock at seeing the email only served to confirm that he was as surprised as we were. Now, sadly, I could see that, once he had the terrible burden of knowledge, he also wished that it were not so. And, although he tried to read it as having some more benign meaning, there was no getting away from the combined sentiment towards us.

We debated for some time what would be the likely outcome of various scenarios, like some toppled chess grand master planning every move in what looked to be his last endgame, from sacrificing the Queen (me), to resignation by toppling the King piece (my husband and the game).

But every move signalled ignominy and eventual checkmate for us. We were the weaker partners, not only in shareholding. With the two main partners in cahoots, plus one of the other minor ones as the advocate of our demise, we could do nothing to prevent anything they had planned for us from happening. It was only the manner of our defeat which we could potentially choose how our inescapable deaths would ensue.

We twisted and turned like suffocating white mice condemned to an agonising death in the medical lab's killing jar, or a sad butterfly specimen impaled with the pin to be destined for some private collection or museum display case. But it was to no avail. Eventually we came to the sickening decision that the only way we could, if not escape our humiliating exodus from our dream, which had truly turned into Dante's hell, was to try and save a tiny piece of our dignity and pride, by electing to resign on the arrival of the South African partners before the start of the board meeting. By choosing to pursue this pre-emptive strike, my husband was seeking to protect me first and foremost from the inevitable character assassination that had undoubtedly been planned, but he had honourably decided to fall on his sword as well.

The next couple of weeks were simply awful as we contemplated the fall to earth that signified the death knell on our dream, while attempting to carry on at work as if nothing were amiss. You can imagine each minute and hour of every day was like a waking nightmare.

The dreadful reality of our situation was clear; we had no likelihood of finding any alternative employment in the relatively small town where we had made our home in the house on the lake. Allied to that, my husband's work visa only applied while he was working for a sponsor company and, when that endorsement was removed, it left us with no choice but to return to the UK.

With my husband no longer able to work, and me having no authorisation to work at all, I would soon to be considered an illegal immigrant if I outstayed the period of three months that a visitor visa would allow. We did contemplate, as perhaps many had before us in similar yet not so dire circumstances, flying out of the country and back in again every three months, but could we afford that expense with no employment and income?

Also, the prospect of staying in that place where everything we looked at was a terrible reminder of our shattered hopes and achievements and perhaps being forced to endure gloating over our demise made it simply untenable to remain.

Every time I looked at our only family we had brought there, our two cats, I cried at what was to become of them. Their fate had been sealed some five years before, when we brought them with us to the USA, as we had resolved that this last relocation was to be a one-way trip for them only. We had decided this (never thinking we would ever have to consider the alternative), because we didn't want to entertain the prospect of them having to endure not only another horrible and distressing plane trip, but after that, a further six months quarantine when we disembarked back in the rabies free UK. However, left all alone as no longer young cats, but aged around 15 years old, we were not sure how they would survive. We were unsure of the exact age of one of them as we had adopted him as a stray, but he had been with us many years. Cats can live to around 25, if they remain free from disease, but he was showing some warning signs of kidney problems as we noticed that he had started to drink copious amounts of water over the last year. Our other cat had nearly died after her journey coming over, as she suffered a dangerous, and no doubt very painful urinary tract infection on her arrival. We had put this down to the fact we discovered when she arrived, that as she had been provided with no water in her crate on the nearly 48-hour journey from the starting point in the UK to eventual collection by us. However, we were unsure if this was indeed the cause or just having had to hold her bladder for the long journey (cats being by nature clean animals not wanting to soil themselves or their immediate surroundings).

We tried not to think about it, but it weighed heavy on our minds that we would have to kill our children (which is how we thought of them).

The housing market was also not brisk as we were poised unfortunately at the start of yet another housing crisis, as always seemed to be our bad luck. This time it was the one caused by the mortgage subprime debacle therefore the uncertainty surrounding this made the market stagnant at best. And even if we sold it, property values had simply dropped through the floor, so we would be unlikely to recover our investment.

We knew that it would cost a hefty sum to ship back our furniture and belongings but, with no employment secured, this time we did not have the option of starting again from scratch. We were also aware that most of the electrical equipment would be a problem, as we would have to step up the voltage from the 120V that the US used to the 240V current in the UK. We did have some transformers that we had purchased for some equipment we had taken with us that could switch both ways, but our massive (for that time) 48-inch TV flatscreen would simply never work due to differences in the program transmission protocols.

We contemplated where we would stay when back in the UK while looking for accommodation and employment and were plagued with a million and one other worries and considerations.

We decided that we would offer a three-month notice period to allow a controlled handover and transition of the business, as we did not want to cause any upset or issues on that side but knew that we could do virtually nothing regarding any significant arrangements to restart our own personal lives until we were back in the UK.

How very noble that decision was from us, especially when you find out what happened after we told the partners we were leaving to return to the UK. Although our actions were not all magnanimous, as we still had our shares and thought that they would allow us at least some small amount of money to return to England. This of course meant that we were motivated not to destroy or devalue what we had worked so hard to earn. Allied to that, we had loyalty both to the employees, and to our friend who, having a shareholding in the company, had often said his pension depended on it securing his retirement pot. We would have had that on our conscience if we had knowingly jeopardised that.

CHAPTER NINETEEN

THE LIE

Finally, the dreaded day came for the arrival of the shareholders into town; we sent an email to all shareholders while they were en route, saying that we would like everyone to come to our house on that first day. We agonised over the wording, as we wanted to not give our intentions away. We hoped that if we, in essence, took the decision that we would simply volunteer to "go quietly", without any need for them to do anything but to gracefully accept it, then allow a controlled, gentlemanly hand-over to take place, they would also be happy about this. We thought that this would be a nice way out for everyone and would avoid the kind of unpleasantness we knew would inevitably transpire if we left it in their hands.

The request for the impromptu meeting was not well received, but it was eventually reluctantly agreed that they would all come over, once they had refreshed themselves after the long flight at the US shareholder's house where, once again, they had elected to stay. We presumed that maybe some guilty consciences might lead them to believe that our request was a little odd, but we wanted to make our announcement on neutral home territory, and in an informal and courteous way that might fit the way friends and business partners would do it.

We asked our friend to arrive early as moral support for the announcement, and in his capacity as a minority shareholder, and so did not think that it would be considered out of order in any way.

We awaited the arrival of the friends of Carlotta, with table and chairs arranged, and drinks laid out in readiness on our deck looking over the lake.

The anticipation of what was to come made the wait almost unbearable, but just as we finally saw the Lexus with Tinker; Tailor & Brutus, drive up to the house, we noticed that, once they spotted the car of our true friend already parked on our drive, they promptly did a U-turn and drove away again.

After a few minutes had passed, with our nerves close to breaking point, we received a call via the US shareholder's mobile phone a few minutes later. I think they must all have sensed something was up, as he bluntly asked the why our friend was there. We replied quite legitimately that, if we had something to say, since he was also a shareholder, why would we not have invited him as well.

Of course, to that reply, nothing further could be said, so, after some more excruciating minutes had elapsed, during which a debate must have taken place between the co-conspirators, they eventually returned and parked in our driveway.

My husband showed them in while our friend and I remained on the deck. I think I may well have taken half of one of my precious tablets of Xanax, as I was literally horrified at what we were about to do, but there was no other option or turning back now. Once they all were seated and offered refreshments, I remained standing to try and hang onto my dignity. I was holding myself up through a mixture of willpower and leaning against the balcony edge, as at that point I wanted to just throw myself off it rather than endure what was to come. The tension was palpable and the atmosphere electric, as the incoming posse looked from us to each other in some confusion and indeed some irritation. In fact, it seemed like animosity about the question of why this impromptu meeting had been called.

They declined our drinks offer, as I think they just wanted to hear what we had to say; then came the dreaded question as to what this was all about and why we had called them all there.

For the second time in the space of two weeks, my blood froze to ice in my veins, as the fateful words were spoken by my brave husband; he said that we had decided we would resign from the company and return to the UK giving a few months' notice until January in the New Year, for the changeover period.

Inevitably, they asked why we had come to this decision; and tellingly, I remember all too clearly it was put as: "What has INFORMED this decision". It may have just been a manner of speaking, but to me it implied that they knew that we knew of their intended treachery or might have had some inkling of what had been going on behind our backs.

It confirmed to me without any shadow of doubt that we had been correct in our interpretation of the likely turn of events, and that we only had been unsure as to what exact form had been planned for our exit.

It took all my willpower and resolve to not shout out – "You KNOW why – you horrible disloyal, plotting conspiring bastards and so-called friends!"

But I was forced to hold onto my nerve and resolve to say nothing about our knowledge of what had been plotted. I could only dig my nails into the balcony edge as I was forced to just look impassively ahead while my husband went through with the overly rehearsed lie.

He simply said that we felt that our work was done in building the company and getting it off to a wonderful and stable start and that we now missed England and our family and friends. He also said that their health was becoming a concern and we felt duty bound to be close by. (Actually, this latter part could have been true, as my parents were getting older, and my fathers' health was not good; he had suffered a heart attack and had had some cancer treatment as well).

But their reaction was disappointing and yet another damning confirmation that our fears for the future were not some feverish imagined scenarios. There was not the tiniest attempt from them to try and change our minds, no sad cries of "No, please do stay, we need you!" No, dear readers, if anything there was just compressing of lips on their side and looks cast towards us as if WE were the betrayers. It was sickening, and once again so hurtful to see that the US shareholder even looked at us as if he hated us.

It was truly awful for both of us, and for our friend, who had to stand mute, looking as if he had had no knowledge of this. In truth, I think that everyone knew we must have shared the news with him first, but we were anxious to try and shield him, while still being incredibly grateful for his silent moral support.

I had known in my heart of hearts, and from my deepest intuition that we would not get the volte face and redeeming support that we might have expected had we not seen that email. However, the reaction of the others was the damning evidence and proof that we were indeed not wanted. If that had not been the truth, then at least some attempts would have been made to ask us to stay or to explore the issue.

It remains one of the saddest days in our lives, having seen that crumbling of the friendships which we had treasured and nurtured, and yet through no fault of our own, were now just a dim memory. Now it seemed to have been replaced now by only hate and mistrust.

The meeting broke up quickly after that, and it was resolved that we would discuss the terms of our exit the next day, when back in the office. Once they had departed, leaving us in a crumpled, beaten-down state of despair to analyse what had just transpired and to ask ourselves to confirm the conclusion that we had come to, and the reality of the plot. We needed to ask ourselves one final time if we had we done the right thing in trying to give everyone a dignified way out.

I am sure you can appreciate what a terrible price it was for us to have to just be polite and innocently pretend that everything was above board. Once it was out there, we just felt exhausted with the effort of maintaining the façade and felt that our hearts had been ripped out from our chests. This was made worse by the lack of any kindly, albeit possibly false, understanding words to make it easier for us. No thanks for our efforts or well wishes for our decision to return to our old home. Instead, we just got cold, unfeeling reactions directed towards us, as if we were the enemy.

I would have thought, given the circumstances, that they might have been relieved and would have known that, if it were indeed genuine circumstances that had caused us to want to resign, it would have been an extremely hard decision for us. So, if they had been true friends or kind-hearted people, they would have at least said something comforting.

The next few days were no less stressful as my husband was blind-sided at one of the meetings. I had unwisely confided some weeks earlier in one of my other only friends, confessing I was a little worried that I might be sacked due to some of the prior events I have described and my part in them.

It was to end up being very uncomfortable as she had recounted my conversation with her boss, who in turn, although an innocent party in the plot, was a close friend of Carlotta and who had then, in turn, shared my misgivings with him; it was therefore unpleasantly brought up at the board meeting.

Of course, this was denied that I would think or say such a thing, but it made it much harder to try and make a dignified exit. After we had offered them an easy way out on a plate, and tacitly "agreed to go quietly", I can only say it was just malicious to have aired that in such a public and humiliating way.

Can a person be hounded by their own guilt for the rest of their life? Yes, of course, and I not only suffered a breakdown on my return to the UK, but it also resulted in me contemplating the taking of my own life. It seemed like the only way out of the dreadful nightmare of self-loathing and immolation that haunted me daily (and, to an extent, still does).

After one especially low point, when we had joined our in-laws for a special silver wedding cruise celebration, booked and paid for by them in advance, I confessed to my husband that I had considered throwing myself overboard off the back of the ship.

On hearing my words, he was so upset that he was furious with me and said I should never consider such a selfish act ever again. However, I still have some very dark days of depression and sadness, especially at Christmas, which it is now as I finish writing this tale and am forced to look back at those final dark days and memories.

Our announcement was made in October 2008. This meant that instead of the controlled and graceful exit from the company and country that we had suggested take place after working three months' notice to January 2009, it was not to be. We were summarily told to clear our desks by the end of the week and hand over all the accounting and IT passwords. We were told we would be paid until the end of the year, but it was an agonising time, as we needed the last pay checks to cover our flight home and for the container we had booked for our furniture to follow.

When November's salary seemed to have not been paid at the end of the month as normal, I was forced to humiliate myself by asking for the help of our friend to ensure that the promised salary would be paid. My husband was unaware of this, as he would have had too much pride to ask, but I was desperate as we had no savings, having spent them all on preparing our home in the summer for the sales conference.

CHAPTER TWENTY

FINAL FAREWELLS

Could anything be worse for us than that? Well, yes it could, and it was.

There ensued a truly miserable time in the lead up to Christmas, which we spent packing belongings into boxes. We had taken the cat with the suspected kidney disease to the vet to have him checked out for his ability to survive the trip home and quarantine, but we were still gripped by indecision as to whether it was fair to inflict the flights and six months isolation on them both once again.

The vet had taken bloods and the results showed that he was in early renal failure; and so it was his recommendation that he should not be made to endure the journey and quarantine period, lest he die a painful death in quarantine without us.

Hearing the news that we would be forced to have him put down was the first and only time in over 30 years of marriage that I have ever seen my husband break down and cry. We both sat down stroking our cat in an agony of guilt and sadness, and I felt wretched as I again thought it was my fault for having asked the question.

The container was booked for early January; the day after it had been loaded, after sleeping on the floor in our empty home, we planned to take the taxi to the airport. To avoid unnecessary stress to the cats we had decided that we would take him to the vet to be put to sleep or as I saw it kill him. Fearing that that the other cat might in turn become ill through the ordeal and would be all alone and scared without her lifelong companion on the trip and in quarantine afterwards, we had also taken the terrible decision that we should not put her through the trip either, so her fate had also been sealed by his.

Christmas Day came and went; it was on Boxing Day (which is not celebrated in America), that our other cat, maybe sensing in that uncanny way that they have that something bad was about to happen, allowed fate to take a hand. I awoke early to hear a strange scrabbling noise on the wooden stairs leading to our bedroom on the first floor.

I got out of bed to investigate and was confronted by our little tabby cat dragging herself up the stairs using only her front legs. I rushed to pick her up, but she managed to haul herself up the last step and somehow stagger into our bedroom. There, she crawled into the walk-in wardrobe, which was adjacent to the door. The scrabbling continued. I called my husband in terror and concern; he got out of bed, hurried over and picked her up tenderly to place her on the bottom of the bed on the soft duvet. As we stroked her, trying to comfort her and see what the problem was, she suddenly lost control of her bladder and we both realised that she had had a massive stroke. I rushed to the phone to call the vet and ask if they could come out to see her, but they said they had best assess her at the surgery to give the best treatment. After agreeing to bring her round by car to the surgery a few miles away, my husband picked her up and carried her to the car. Following closely behind I went to open the car door so he could place her on the soft blanket for the short journey, but before I could get there, I saw her suddenly writhe in some terrible death agony, and she twitched one last time. With her eyes still wide open, I saw she was dead.

As my tears fall onto my keyboard, I can only say that we buried her by the lake at the bottom of the garden, by a beautiful tree I had planted that we were destined never to see bloom with its host of pink flowers the following spring.

It was there that we took our black cat a few days later, to bury him next to his companion.

They say that having an animal euthanised is a peaceful event, and that the animal does not suffer anything more than going into a deep sleep. However, the sedative we elected to have him given, to try and make it less stressful for him, made him vomit before he finally slipped away. It seemed that our punishment and sorrow was to have no respite.

After burying him next to the other cat in the garden, in a deep dark depression filled with guilt and remorse, we sorrowfully packed up the rest of our belongings. The container was due the next day.

Do you think that our agonies were to be finally over? Do you think that if there is a God, he had finished punishing us? For what, I am not quite sure, but he was not about to let me off that easily.

I needed to be dealt one final awful blow for the sin of pride, and my husband, who was innocent of any wrongdoing, was also to be made to pay in another way before we were finally allowed to leave.

We were anxious for the air conditioning bill not to continue to cripple us with more expense after we had left, while the house was empty and on the market for sale.

Consequently, my husband had decided, prompted by me, to close the basement air vents. He stood on a small table to reach it, but it collapsed suddenly under him. After picking himself up, he discovered that he had painfully broken one of his fingers. So it was, that after the truly anguishing day's events, he then lay awake all night in immense physical pain. As we could not afford to hire proper movers, he also had the prospect of having to load up all the boxes and our heavy furniture the next day with a broken finger.

Even after taking a combination of some extremely strong pain killers, I had left over after an operation I had had, mixed with a huge amount of red wine, we could not manage to assuage the awful pain he was in.

After that sleepless night, he had to load all the boxes onto the container with his finger taped up and in a huge amount of pain as he lifted each box and piece of heavy furniture onto it with only the help of our loyal ex-warehouse man to assist. It was awful to watch my husband's obvious physical pain allied to his emotional hurt from having to destroy our beloved cat.

If like me, you can hardly stand for me to go on, I will end with just two final curtains on the whole affair, so I can hopefully cry just one last time, before closing the book at last.

The first of my horrible revelations came on that last day, as we awaited the arrival of our taxi to the airport. I had decided I would go down to the garden to bid my cats' graves a last farewell and to once again try and beg their forgiveness.

But I was denied even a tiny bit of support in that last act of sorrow, because, as my husband and I were about to do down together, our friend, the young sales assistant, arrived at the front door to say goodbye to us.

While he went down to the graves on his own, I was forced to stay a while to bid her thanks for all her help, to give her a final tearful hug and give her some vases, our bread-maker she had admired, and some other bits and pieces that just would not fit into the container, so I thought she might as well have them.

Once she had gone, it was left for me to go down to the graves alone to say goodbye to my cats.

When I reached the site, I was beside myself in floods of tears and remorse, literally sinking to my knees on the damp ground next to the twin graves in sorrow. Then finally, knowing that the taxi would be arriving any minute now, I eventually gathered myself together and got to my feet to make the weary, dejected trudge back up the hill through my once treasured garden.

But it was at this moment I thought I heard a piteous miaow.

My god, I thought, we have buried him alive! I turned back and listened hard in anguish, debating whether to start scrabbling at the soil over the grave with my bare hands to see if this was the truth. Can you imagine anything worse than that moment?

I hesitated, totally torn between the rational part of my last vestiges of sanity and control, which were saying I surely must have imagined it. The vet would not have made a mistake like that, and he must surely be dead after having been buried for at least a day. But then I also thought, "What if I find he had come back to life?" Maybe the strong anaesthetic had not been enough to kill my brave cat who had survived for so long, first as an unwanted stray and after enduring three international flights and six months in quarantine as well? If so, when I disinterred him covered in soil and barely alive what could I do? Strangle him with my bare hands? Drown him in the lake?

I screamed out loud in anguish at the horrific thoughts, then heard my husband calling that the taxi was here. In an agony of indecision, I had to leave the graveside. I sobbed uncontrollably as I dragged myself one last time, dejected and completely distraught, back up the hillside to the waiting taxi.

Looking back, I have reasoned, albeit with little comfort, that it must have been a crow shrieking, or some other neighbour's cat I had heard. Even after my husband assured me that he was most certainly lifeless when he was buried, the tiny doubt remains. I hope and pray to God that maybe it was my terrible conscience, and me being demented with grief that had caused my mind to play some final horrible trick on me, but still there remains that nagging doubt that I should have gone back to check. If I had plucked up the courage, or if fate had not made it so that my friend had delayed me, or if the taxi had not then arrived, maybe it would have allowed me the time to have dug him up, so at least I would have been sure that we had not actually buried our cat alive.

Surely this is the worst of anyone's nightmares; so many times, since that decision I have thought that perhaps, if I had been able to perform this final check, while I still would have felt guilty and sad, I might have been spared the years of regret and self-immolation.

Despite all the rest that happened, even losing our friends, business and, eventually, our home, it is this that remains the deepest scar on my soul, which will haunt me to my dying day.

CHAPTER TWENTY-ONE

ONE LAST KICK & FINAL JUDGEMENT

So, I can bring this story to its conclusion, and then perhaps finally allow my soul some rest and move on.

On our return to the UK during the turbulent and less than auspicious start of 2009, we still had many trials and tribulations to deal with as we fought to get our lives back. Arriving, as we did, at the worst possible time to be looking for a job, and with no source of income until we had found some employment, there remained not one, but two final cruel kicks, which would finally crush and extinguish for good the last vestiges of our dream.

In order that we could properly start again from scratch, we needed to raise a deposit for a house, but we were finding it increasingly hard as we were struggling to pay rent in the UK, while at the same time maintaining the mortgage payments on our house in the US. In the end we took the decision to sell our shares, but we were forced to accept a much-reduced value compared to what we believed they should have been worth. According to the rule of seven or eight times the company valuation, as we read it, it could have been a lifesaver, but of course, after all our years of blood, sweat and tears, we were offered a much lower and rather insulting amount according to the valuation made by the friends' accountant. I suppose they knew that we had no choice to accept what they offered.

Although we felt we had been cheated, we agreed to take the amount proffered so we could, at least, finally close the door on the whole sad affair, and hang onto our house and the equity invested in it until such time as we were able to sell it. Or so we thought.

However, even with the money we got from the reluctant sale of our shares, after months of paying for rented accommodation in the UK while continuing to pay the loan on our house in America, we just could not afford to sustain the payments. We had tried unsuccessfully to sell the house in the aftermath of the financial crash, but once the last tenants had moved out, we had in desperation tried to hold off the inevitable by renting it; we finally had to regretfully allow it to be repossessed by the bank, losing all our equity in the process.

I am sorry if you were hoping for a happy-ever-after Disney ending to this torrid tale of woe and misfortune, but our ex-partners had just one more final kick in the teeth for us.

We found out a short while after we had been forced to sell out our shares based on the low valuation made at that time, that only a few years later, probably at the highest point of its eventual sales turnover, having become established in all the remaining independent running stores, the company was sold out, at what I believe was an enormous profit for the remaining shareholders.

The irony of this was that the buy-out was from none other than the franchise chain and major customer who had sought to control our supply.

If you remember at the start of my tale, I had voiced early doubts about the suspected "mole" introduced from that company. At the time the suggestion had been vilified as being totally without substance.

Later, that company had sought to take control of our stock and operations, which I had also resisted strongly, much to the annoyance of the other partners. I believed this signified our fall from grace. Perhaps the outcome gives weight and justification to my "conspiracy theory"?

I leave it up to you to decide, I do not mind being judged.

If indeed I brought this all down upon us, I believe I have paid a very heavy price for sticking to what I believed were my principles. In the end, I am not sure whether, if I had the chance to do it all over again, anything would have turned out differently. People are ultimately who they are and maybe they can never change.

POSTSCRIPT

There is one last piece of the puzzle that truly ends my story. You can then be the ultimate judge and decide if indeed we were conspired against all along, or if we could have avoided our eventual fate and destruction.

I was contacted unexpectedly several years ago on a business networking site. I was surprised to see that it was from none other than one of the ex-partners who was unbelievably asking if we could still be friends.

There was no admission of guilt, nor was any apology made or even remorse expressed for what had been done to us.

I wrestled with my conscience, trying desperately to find something within me that would allow me to forgive, and trying to believe that, after all, perhaps it had not been any pre-meditated intention that culminated in the awful treachery and betrayal. I reasoned with myself that it would be the "Christian" or nice and right thing to do.

However, in the end, I knew that I would need to first forgive them before I could bring myself to re-establish our old friendship. I realised that, even if I could bring myself to extend that hand, my husband never would and nor did I have any right to ask him to.

I therefore concluded that, without sufficient apology being offered, since we were still suffering the horrible consequences of their actions, while I felt bad that I could not grant that forgiveness, I could only respond that, "After all that had happened, I was unable to be friends with them again."

But in a misery of emotions, I continued to be conflicted by my decision, as the memories of the happy times of the early days of our friendship came flooding back.

However, as I battled with myself, my reticence was in the end vindicated. Their reply was the almost unbelievably hypocritical and pious recommendation that I should not "live in hate", and that "it was always going to end the way it did".

Forgiveness may be divine, and victims of war or violent crime may be able to offer it. I am in awe of their humanity for being able to, but should I also offer that comfort and balm to a friend unless they first show that they are genuinely sorry for their actions? After all that had happened, and especially after that admission? I am not sure about you, but I was not prepared to give anything, least of all forgiveness.

Perhaps we will all burn in hell together, but I think I already have.

Time for my martini methinks. I think I will make it an extra-large one tonight…

Printed in the United States
by Baker & Taylor Publisher Services